*Your life, Your Future
Never Quit*

SUCK LESS, DO BETTER

Suck Less, Do Better

The End of Excuses & the Rise of the Unstoppable You

Nate Green

©2024 All Rights Reserved. No portion of this book may be reproduced, stored in a retrieval system, or transmitted in any form or by any means-electronic, mechanical, photocopy, recording, scanning, or other-except for brief quotations in critical reviews or articles without the prior permission of the author.

Published by Game Changer Publishing

Paperback ISBN: 978-1-963793-96-3
Hardcover ISBN: 978-1-963793-97-0
Digital ISBN: 978-1-963793-98-7

www.GameChangerPublishing.com

Dedication

To my parents, you have been the greatest examples of how to grow and succeed despite any hardships, adversity, and obstacles. You both are truly unstoppable forces who have shown up and have always striven to become the best versions of yourselves regardless of your circumstances.

Dad, you went from being a high school dropout to earning multiple master's degrees and a PhD, leading in both colleges and ministries. I will always admire, appreciate, and hope to follow in your footsteps as a leader, father, Christian, and wise counsel.

Mom, you have set an amazing example of patience, love, and support throughout my life. Even while working through the most traumatic challenges and hardships anyone should ever face, you used them to maximize your impact, supporting others through their trauma. The lives you both lead, and the great examples you set have profoundly impacted me beyond words.

You have both demonstrated through your examples and leadership that life comes with hardships, difficulties, challenges, and obstacles, but it is our responsibility to leverage every opportunity to better ourselves and always show up as the best version of who we are meant to be.

I love you both and could not be more grateful for the way you raised me with love and support, providing the right guidance when I tested the boundaries. Thank you both for your dedication to me and our family, always striving to be the best versions of yourselves.

Your Son,
Nate

To my son, Caleb, my dude, there is not a day that goes by that I do not thank God that I get to be your dad. I am blessed to have you as a part of my life and to walk some of our crazy roads together. With all your energy and excitement, coupled with your love and care for others, I look forward to the ongoing development of who you are becoming.

The day I first held you, I knew my life would never be the same. I hope and pray that I show you each day how much I love you. I know I am not perfect, but always know that I am working to better myself every day, even how I parent. You are at the core of my driving force that keeps me pushing forward and constantly working to better myself.

As I wrote this book and as I continue to develop into the greatest version of who I am called to be, I hope to be an example for you and an inspiration to always grow, learn, develop and overcome obstacles in your journey.

You are one of a kind and you are built exactly how you were meant to be. The future that is in front of you is whatever you make of it. I am proud of you and proud to be your father.

I love you,
Dad

Read This First

What a journey you are on, moving through life trying to figure out the success, goals or achievements you can reach. The process of facing each day striving and hungry for a better future can be relentless. The life you have in front of you is filled with potential and possibility, but it requires you to take the actions required. I know where you are at, and I have been in your shoes. To be honest, I am still in that same situation, I still believe the best version of who I can become is in process and in my future. Through this book I am hoping to be a part of your journey and a part of your development. I am laying out principles and action steps that I have personally used throughout my life to gain major success. I set out to have an impact in other people's lives and never focused on only finding success for myself.

As a thank you for buying and reading this book, I am providing some additional resources and downloads for your development. These are all available to give more direction and guidance for your future success. Use the QR code below or go to www.SuckLessDoBetterBook.com/Resources

Scan the QR Code Here:

Suck Less, Do Better

*The End of Excuses & the Rise
of the Unstoppable You*

Nate Green

www.GameChangerPublishing.com

Table of Contents

Introduction – To Settle or To Rise 1

Chapter 1 – Define Your Suck 11

Chapter 2 – Your Lens Is Broken 21

Chapter 3 – Write Your Story, Not Mine 37

Chapter 4 – Ignite Your Driving Forces 47

Chapter 5 – Hyperfocus on You 65

Chapter 6 – Set Your Lighthouse 81

Chapter 7 – The Truth of Your Reality 97

Chapter 8 – Identify Your Competition 113

Chapter 9 – Foundation for Momentum 127

Chapter 10 – Suck Less, Do Better Every Day 139

Conclusion – Live in Your Suck or Succeed 153

INTRODUCTION

To Settle or To Rise

The doctor cleared his throat as he prepared to deliver the news that I would never be the same. He told me that they had determined that I was dealing with a degenerative condition with my heart, and he expressed his concern for a shortened life as well as extreme difficulties in my future. This blow was more than a hit to my identity as a police officer—it was an awakening of fear and a hard reality that I had to face. With the thoughts racing in my head at that moment, it was impossible to understand the unexpected reality he was communicating to me and fully connect with the outcome and concerns he was explaining.

I had been working with many doctors and going through so many tests to determine the cause of the health issues I had been dealing with. This news wasn't the expected outcome and didn't make sense given the timeline and the symptoms I had faced. I felt as though they had no other explanation or medical answer, so they were going with specific markers or escalations to determine the stated degenerative issues. I expressed my concern and bit back with some snarky statements that I hoped would lead this doctor to explore other potential causes or explanations.

The mental anguish I experienced each day following that appointment left me stuck in my thoughts. My headspace was a gauntlet of hardship and daily anguish as I wrestled with this news and worked through the following months of additional testing. I had to determine who I was going to be and how I was going to show up despite the results and outcome. I was dealing with a significant problem with my heart and had to determine what my life was now going to look like. I wasn't willing to give in to the feelings of wanting to throw in the towel or settle further into the depression I was fighting each day. It was time to dig deep and determine how I needed to show up every day to get myself through this situation and set myself up for the best future.

As you walk through your life, I can guarantee you will be hit with hard truths, difficulties, uphill battles, mental grinding, and tough decisions. You can either rise to the occasion or settle for less challenging roads. Those who are hungry for success, growth, and achieving their goals understand that if you settle, you will be left with an unquenchable thirst. You have to determine whether you will join the crowd on the easy road or rise up and become the greatest version of yourself. It's time for you to make the decision to "suck less, do better" within your specific situation and keep chasing success despite any hardships you encounter.

The entire reason I wrote this book is for you—yes, just for you and this exact moment. I might not know who you are, but I can connect with your struggles and even some of the same difficulties that you have or are facing. My goal for this book is to be a guide in your life, a support for this part of your journey, and, more importantly, a catalyst to help you achieve the future you're chasing. I wrote this book for those of you who are hungry, driven, and motivated. Some of you have faced or are facing major challenges in your life, and others are wishing for more results and a better future. This book is a complete guide on how to get out of your own way and connect the core aspects of what will be the foundation of your future success.

I have structured this book very strategically, and you'll have to go through some challenging chapters in the beginning to get to the more exciting aspects of the planning and action. The groundwork in the first few chapters will require you to reflect and work through some "holdbacks" that too many individuals never confront. As a result, they fail to achieve the greatest version of who they can become. I intend to help you get to the most excellent version of who you can become and achieve the highest success. I call your goals, ambitions, and who you are going to be your "lighthouse." You have to chase after this with a relentless spirit, always ready for action and dedicated to constantly improving who you are.

Your Crossroads

You are sitting at your crossroads right now, and two different versions of you can emerge in this next phase of your life. You can choose either the complacent, settled, comfort-seeking, easy-road-chasing, and excuse-making version or the relentless, hungry, dedicated, challenge-facing, risk-taking, reality-checking, and constantly adapting version. You must decide which version you want to live and what you want to be known for. You must identify what you are called to become and what you will take on during your journey. What are you driven, motivated, and dedicated to chasing down? How do you want your story to read at the end of your journey?

The right choice for you is the one that forces you to grow, strengthens you, and produces the greatest version of who you can become. Are you willing to do the required hard work and take on what life throws at you? Life will bring difficulties and hardships, and you must stay dedicated to identifying how you will show up and proceed down the difficult road to becoming excellent. Your goals, ambitions, and who you are driven to become are the "lighthouse" guiding your journey.

Unstoppable success will come only after you have channeled all the vital elements of who you are and unlocked your full potential. *There are no shortcuts, and there are no simple paths.* It's all about how prepared, how ready, and how willing you are to take on life's challenges despite any difficulties you face and how you can thrive through the process. At this point, you'll have to stop making excuses—your future no longer allows you to sit around and lick your wounds. Your future will come, and it's up to you how you'll show up and how prepared you'll be. This life you're living doesn't have a reset button. You have only one opportunity to chase after the greatest version of yourself and reach the lighthouse you set for yourself. As you're sitting here at the crossroads, you must accept the fact that at the end of your journey, there will be no one else to blame but you. *The decision to take ownership of your life and your future is yours alone to make.*

Life is a Journey

Life is all about the journey—the learning, growing, and developing as we get through each situation that we're challenged with. Hardships and obstacles are all a required part of this journey, and there is absolutely no escaping them. However, you do get to make daily choices on how you will handle yourself through all the challenges and hardships you're faced with. The way you handle situations will have an impact on you forever and determine the outcome of your life. The way you go after your obstacles will determine what you become. The way you chase down your goals, ambitions, and relationships will be the story you remember on your deathbed, either with regrets or satisfaction with the legacy you are leaving behind.

Connection to My Journey

As a part of my life journey and even writing this book, it's essential for me to be open about some problematic areas of my life and the arduous journey I've taken. The life I've lived has not been exempt from difficulties or hardships but rather filled with what seemed to be impossible challenges and kicks to the face. Yet, I still remain dedicated to showing up every day as the best version of myself. I've learned throughout the adversities, difficulties, and troubled times that I have to constantly push myself to succeed. I have to chase down the greatest version of myself. I am the one in control of how I show up each day and how I handle all of the challenges on my journey. I am hungry, driven, motivated, and relentless in chasing my lighthouse, the most excellent version of who I can become and the highest success I am built to achieve.

Growing up, I wasn't born or raised with a silver spoon in my mouth. I was brought up in a lower-income family, with my father working himself through the ministry and the school system. Living in a single-income household, I watched my dad work hard and push relentlessly to provide for his family and grow himself as a leader. My mom wore her patience to the bone as she worked to raise the four of us kids. We constantly tested her sanity while she tried to keep us all from killing each other.

When I was almost fifteen, my dad sat me down and explained that he would always be here to support me in life, provide guidance, and be a shoulder I could lean on for wisdom and direction. He let me know that I would always have a roof over my head, whether I was working full time or in school full time, but there were some things that he wouldn't be able to provide. If I wanted a car when I turned sixteen, then I needed to get a job when I was fifteen. If I was going to get a car, I had to make sure I had the money available for insurance, repairs, and fuel. He explained that going to college and getting an education was very important, but I would have to rely on scholarships and my own hard-earned money to go to college. My dad prepared me mentally for what adulthood would look like financially and didn't hide the reality of our family's financial situation. He had worked hard to provide for all of our needs, but there was a transition of responsibility when it came to conveniences, experiences, higher education, and other nonessentials.

During middle and high school, I definitely was not voted "most likely to succeed." In fact, my name was nowhere on that list and probably on some other lists that most wouldn't want to be on. Getting mocked and picked on was a constant theme in my life during those tough years. I know the inner scars that come from those developmental years, and a part of this book will help you connect with and work to repair those deep-rooted hurts so that you can thrive despite your scars. My stories are here and laced throughout the book to connect with each of you and give you a feel for the challenges that I have faced, and help you understand my vantage point and deep-rooted hunger to overcome limits and conquer obstacles.

When I was nineteen, I was hired as a police officer after putting myself through the police academy. Because of this career path, I was faced with severe trauma on a regular basis. I earned the nickname "Dr. Death" in my first three months on the job, so you can imagine what I had to deal with as a nineteen-year-old. Luckily, after taking some severe beatings—and giving some out—my nickname quickly changed to "Rook Nasty" and stuck throughout the rest of my career as a cop.

This job was exciting, invigorating, and a constant enjoyable challenge for me, but there were risks and dangers. While in my police cruiser, I was in a bad car accident that left me paralyzed for a few months. After recovering from the paralysis, I developed a major heart problem that left me unable to continue my journey as a police officer. The transition was unexpected, unwelcome, and a rude awakening. I had to retire my gun and my badge, and I lost a part of who I was at age twenty-three. I still have a vivid memory of the day they announced over the dispatch radio that Officer Nathan Green, "Rook Nasty," forever 10-7 (out of service).

Because I refused to give up and always strived to grow, learn, and develop, I adapted and set off on my plan to launch a business. During this next phase, I focused on learning about sales. I had been let go from the police force with no retirement, severance, or any other monetary assistance, but I refused to accept any government aid as I knew I was still capable of earning a living. I wasn't going to let myself sit in the house and wallow in my hurt and devastation. I launched my first business in 2008 and almost immediately thereafter fell into financial difficulty—which nearly led me to file for personal bankruptcy. However, I showed up every day to turn things around, and I built it into an award-winning business that was acquired for eight figures.

At the time when I was transitioning from my career as a cop and experiencing medical challenges in my life, I met the woman who would later become my wife. Our ten-year marriage was extremely tough and required a lot of self-work to recover from when it ended. Due to legal restrictions, I'm not able to share the details of this part of my journey and how it led to trauma therapy for me and my kids.

After this, my life's second abrupt transition, I became a single dad with full custody for years before I met my current wife, who has been a great blessing to all of us. Through the many challenging years, hard lessons, and difficulties I went through, I have been able to rise to the occasion and am continually driven to discover the greatest version of myself.

The reason I give you these past glimpses of my life and open up throughout this book is to make sure you have a baseline understanding of who I am, the disasters I've been through, and what I'm made of. You need to be aware of the hard grind I'm willing to go through in my life to achieve great results. I start each day focused on showing up for my family, dedicating myself to my career, reaching my lighthouse, and keeping my eye on the potential impact I can have in the lives of people just like you. I understand that when you're in the middle of hardships and trauma, it's not easy to gain inspiration from someone who has not seen the kind of challenges you're facing. When I made the decision to write this book, I knew it would require me to be open, honest, and vulnerable to have the kind of effect I set out to achieve. For myself, my family, my future, and for you, I am committed to always suck less and do better as I continue on my journey.

Your Journey and Your Guide

If you're on a mission to hit your goals, achieve success, and discover the best version of yourself, then it's time to dig in and push forward. It's time to chase after your lighthouse. It doesn't matter what challenges you are facing or have faced. You need to connect with the principles and mindsets that move you forward and help you become the unstoppable force you're meant to be. This book was developed and written to help you gain clarity and understand that you were built for a greater purpose than you are allowing yourself. The following chapters will guide you to understand the core foundation needed to reach your full potential and become the unstoppable version of you. You cannot allow yourself to settle into comfort and complacency, stifling the person you can become. You must have the right mindset and work through the daily steps to find the success you crave. The process laid out for you in this book, if followed, will unlock the core elements necessary for you to charge forward without hesitation and chase hard after your clearly identified lighthouse.

Movement just for the sake of movement is never going to break you out of your suck and get you to the future that you're built for. You must have a plan—focused intentions, specific goals, ambitions, and actions—to set you on the road to your best future. Impulse-based action will lead you to failure, distractions, and burnout. Planning and setting the right goals, along with your drive and hunger, is the formula for your success. Your future demands that you connect with who you are, what your driving forces are, your goals, and the actions you need to take. This is your journey, and you have to decide whether you're ready to achieve success and become the best version of yourself.

Is This Book for You?

Who is this book *not* for? Let's start there. This book is definitely not written for those who want to continue making excuses for their lack of action and results. It's not for people who wish to continue to live in the hurt of their past versus overcoming their trauma, pain, and issues. It's not for individuals who are satisfied with a complacent life and "normal" results and don't care about finding their true potential. Those who let their fears, insecurities, and inner demons win or those who are looking for the easy road versus battling to hit their full potential.

My purpose in writing this book is to help you get out of your own way, but just reading this book is not enough. Work will be required. Your future calls for you to take different steps to break away from the cycle that's holding you back. Your future demands your full participation, dedication, and action. It's up to you to stop making excuses. If you're resistant to the truth, tough love, and removing excuses, then this book will be just another time filler and another failure to make progress on your list.

So, who *is* this book for? This book is written and dedicated to the hungry, driven, and motivated individuals who want to better themselves. Those who show up by learning, growing, and adapting. Those who are determined to find the best version of themselves. Those who don't let life's difficulties, hardships, and obstacles conquer them. Those who think that "good enough" isn't enough and want to become great. Those set on becoming unstoppable in their journey. Those who know that they just need the proper guidance, encouragement, and direction to hit their goals.

Some of you might already have several of the right tools and maybe even a good foundation, but parts of the equation are missing. If you apply the principles in this book and do the work I challenge you to do, it will have a massive impact on your future success. Use the book as a guide and a catalyst to design your roadmap and your lighthouse, and I have no doubt that you will find the greatest version of yourself.

The Catalyst

The first part of this book is intended to push you hard and uncover all of your holdbacks. It may feel at times like you should have put on scuba gear because of how deep we're diving. In Chapter 4, I'll let you come up for air and transition into the more exciting part of the work to be done. There are direct and pointed statements throughout the book, some of which might not apply to you, but use them for self-reflection and to determine whether there are any related holdbacks in your life. Work through all the core-building aspects I'm going to walk you through to get the right foundation in place. The process is intended to remove your excuses, eliminate what's holding you back, and leave you free to chase after your success. This part of your journey, with these principles and foundations as your guide, should be the defining moment and a catalyst for the rise of an unstoppable you.

To provide you with support throughout your process, I have created additional resources, including videos and downloads. You can access them by visiting www.SuckLessDoBetterBook.com/Resources or scanning the QR Code below.

CHAPTER 1

Define Your Suck

You feel it. You know it's deep inside of you, but you're not sure what to do with it. It's a never-ending restlessness that keeps you unsettled and makes you not know what you should be doing or doing differently. There's an internal hunger and drive, but there are fears, insecurities, and so many other holdbacks that leave you crippled and feeling like you're not showing up in the way you're meant to be showing up. This is part of what I refer to as your "suck." It's time to take your life head-on and define what your suck is— and then charge in the opposite direction. The charge must be with purpose, direction, and dedication, but it starts with knowing what you're running from and what you need to escape. You have to start taking action despite the unknowns and your inability to control every aspect of your life. Your future is defined by your choices and actions today. *Either you can let your suck define who you are, or you can break free and write the story of your future and success.*

As I made the choice to keep planning, chasing, and driving hard to better my life and future, I was still facing additional tests and results from the cardiologist. I worked through a process of looking at what I was determined to become and how I was going to show up in my life. The only thing I knew for sure was that I had to show up each day with grit and determination and set goals for my entire life despite the timeline the doctors had discussed. I had to dig deep throughout this journey and show up in a way that, at the time, felt impossible. The seasons of our lives are full of hardships and unknowns, but we can control our response to these challenges. I knew I was deep in the hurt locker. I was facing more unknowns than I had ever encountered before. The looming medical issue could cripple any plans I put in place, but it made me more determined than ever.

I spent countless hours determining who I was meant to be, how I was supposed to show up, and what I was really meant to become on this crazy journey of life. It kept me up at night more than the news I had received from the doctors. The fire in me was ignited when I was young and has never been extinguished. Now, sixteen years later and with more achievements under my belt than I expected, I'm still restless. That fire still wakes me up early every morning and pushes me to constantly better the entrepreneur, dad, husband, and son that shows up each and every day. I have a hunger in me that will never be filled and will always drive me to be there for the people in my life. I have never and will never allow myself to be stuck in the suck. I'll identify the suck that I'm running from, and then suck less and do better every day.

Your suck is personal. It's the complacency and comfort and the fears, insecurities, and excuses that keep you from becoming the best version of yourself. You must do the work and determine precisely what your suck looks like. This will require you to work through the deep-rooted aspects of your life and push yourself to be open to the process. American poet and playwright E. E. Cummings wrote, "It takes courage to grow up and become who you really are." Maybe you feel that you're already showing up and thriving, but the process of working through these deep-rooted aspects will be the difference between simply finding success versus achieving your greatest success and becoming who you're really meant to be. This journey is not easy and will require you to be open with yourself as well as work through some deep-seated holdbacks, hardships, and difficulties.

Definition Through Reality

This process requires you to be honest with yourself, and many times, people don't want to face that reality. You need to define your suck, not anybody else's. Dig into your reality—not the surface-level things, but the deep-rooted things that are moving you toward your suck versus helping you identify your greatness. The more open and honest you are about your suck, the greater the long-term outcome you'll be able to achieve.

There is no shortcut to defining your suck and your lighthouse, and there are going to be moments when you want to shut down and crawl back into the comfort zone that will become your suck. This process isn't easy, and you'll have to open the closets, uncover the hurt, identify the struggles, and look at all your holdbacks. You will have to face the parts of your life that drive you back toward your suck rather than allowing you to chase your future based upon the greatest version of who you can become.

An ongoing process is required to make sure your decisions and your actions are always moving you forward toward your lighthouse and not allowing you to fall back into your suck. John C. Maxwell, thought leader and best-selling author, says, "Change is inevitable. Growth is optional." You have to identify and define your suck so you can see each and every movement of your life and determine where the momentum is pushing you. Are your actions propelling you forward toward the most excellent version of you, the greatest success that you can become, your lighthouse? Or are you slipping and falling back toward the complacent, settled, subpar, participation-trophy-accepting version of yourself? No one is exempt from finding themselves in their suck despite their strenuous efforts. That's why you must define what your suck is. It will make the vision of what you are driving hard toward, your lighthouse, clearer.

Unsettled Deep Look

You and I both know we are constantly wrestling with feelings throughout our journey. Many of us aren't very good at communicating and working through them, but they are a deep-rooted part of our drive and ambition. You struggle with this inner fight and feel you're always holding back and not doing enough. You don't know where to direct all this inner hunger, all this desire for achievement and results. You look at your current situation and results and think that this can't be how your greatest success will be defined. This is you trying to break away from your current self to discover who you are really built to be.

What gifts, abilities, and qualities do you have that are being underutilized in your current situation? What inner holdbacks are serving as a ball and chain, constantly holding you back from taking leaps of faith and gaining movement down the path of your journey? Your insecurities? Your fears? False limitations that you're allowing yourself to believe? Or maybe the comforts that you're afraid to walk away from?

Your life will have some or all of these, and despite where you are in your journey or what you have achieved, there will always be these inner demons that can create holdbacks and an inability to see or reach your lighthouse. My life is no different. I have achieved great success and conquered a lot of hardships, but I'm still plagued by the same potential holdbacks. I need to be aware of them and keep the expectations I have for myself focused on my lighthouse and the greatest version of myself that I feel I'm capable of. Each day, I push past my fears, insecurities, frustrations, and hardships. I have a sign in my home office that says, "I will not settle on good. I am called to be *great*." It's my constant reminder that I have to move forward every day despite any feelings or desires to fall back into comfort or security.

I know I am called to push past any hardships, holdbacks, difficulties, challenges, and obstacles to be an example and provide guidance to as many people as I can reach. I have been through a lot and succeeded despite all odds—and I am passionate and dedicated to helping others do the same. Writing this book required me to push past the holdbacks that draw me toward my suck and to take the actions to show up as the better version of who I was able to be. I knew that I had to go beyond my comfort zone, beyond my fears, and beyond my perceived limitations to dedicate myself to having an impact on the lives of those I feel I am called to reach. So, as you're reading this book, know that every day, I am practicing what I'm calling on you to practice. I'm chasing hard every day after the life that I'm telling you to chase after. I am striving and driving hard away from my suck, and that is what I'm pushing you to do.

In this process, you need to be honest with yourself about where you are in your life. Yes, you need to look at your insecurities, your fears, your false limitations, and the comforts that you've allowed to inform your decision-making—but your arrogance, overconfidence, or lack of ability to take criticism and learn from others also play a role. There is a direct connection between arrogance and failure. I have seen many fail due to their inability to learn and adapt. They are more focused on acting like they have it all figured out rather than constantly striving to actually get it all figured out. Your arrogance will become a significant crack in your foundation and actually cause your failure if you don't keep it in check.

Take a good look at your life. Are you living in every success that you have and flaunting it, or are you winning and then focusing on your next goal? Let your actions speak for themselves. Don't throw your success in other people's faces, but rather, learn from the process and allow your development and growth to speak for itself. Working with so many entrepreneurs, I have seen the arrogance and flaunting of one's successes firsthand—and then the road that comes next, filled with failures and a solid slice of humble pie. These are all entrepreneurs and executives with extraordinary abilities and skill sets.

However, the small successes they let go to their heads, the arrogance they allow to creep in, and their inability to adapt, grow, learn, and change becomes the gateway to their failure. I can tell you many stories of real-life situations where people are more focused on trying to *look successful* than doing the work required and grinding through the process to actually *become successful*. Arrogance and teachability cannot live in the same timeline. In your life, look at the small successes. See if you're becoming arrogant and proud and are slowly shutting down your learning ability. If so, your life will head down the path toward failure if you don't get it in check.

To hit your true potential, goals, and greatness, you must remain humble in the process. There's no room for arrogance. If you have enough money to retire, never work again, and have six figures of passive income each year without doing anything—then that is what I call success. Until you hit that mark, you must keep your head down and take in as much information and knowledge as possible. You must continuously drive hard and move forward because there's still a more fantastic version of you to unlock. Even though I have hit these success markers myself and can retire at any moment, I still drive hard to learn at every corner. I'm constantly developing who I am, and I keep chasing the best version of what I can become, adapting based on the needs of my businesses, teams, family, future, and the potential people I can reach in my life.

I refuse to settle on *good* when I'm called to be *great*. This goes beyond financial success. It goes beyond business success and the accolades that come with it. It involves impacting and making a difference in other people's lives. So, no matter what success you think you've achieved in your life, you have not yet hit the greatest version of yourself. To achieve greatness and success and become the person you are called to be, you have to remain in a state of learning and adaptation. You have to have a *sponge* mentality rather than a *rock* mentality. Your business, life, career, and family are always changing and will require you to adapt and learn. You may need to show up in different ways. You might have to adjust to what is required of you to support them rather than being stuck in who you once were. Humility and your ability to adapt and adjust to the needs of those around you will be your greatest asset in this process.

Complacency and Full Potential

You are built for so much more than you're currently allowing yourself to be. If you are not fully connected to your reality and holdbacks, it will be impossible to unlock your full potential. Settling for the easy road will never fulfill your deep-rooted hunger. Not living up to what you are built for and built to be is a huge part of your subpar expectations of yourself and will lead to your suck. Notice that I didn't say "born to be," I said "built to be." Each of us is born with an innate characteristic of who we are at our core, but we're in a constant state of development and can grow, learn, and adapt throughout life. The challenges and difficulties in life will derail your progress and development unless you relentlessly charge forward and never let the easy roads, simple paths, complacency, and security pull you back toward the suck that you know you need to run from.

Realizing you are called to be so much more than you are now is something that every highly driven, motivated, and dedicated individual wrestles with. Some may feel an unsettled spirit inside because they know that what they've accomplished thus far is only a drop in the bucket compared to what they're capable of achieving. Who you are—the aggregate of your potential, talent, skills, and abilities—is nothing without the dedication to become great. Where are you failing yourself? Why are you not allowing yourself to run with the abilities you've been given? Where are you falling short and not pushing yourself to the level you know you should be able to reach? Where are you allowing your suck to be so comfortable that you forget that your lighthouse can be achieved through the discomfort of development and growth? Where are you falling back rather than pushing forward to the future you can create? Thoughts of your full potential should be a major driving force to commit to showing up each day as someone who will move relentlessly toward achieving a better future.

All of us have had difficulties and hardships in the past. Trauma, drama, issues, and insecurities can hold us back from seeing and becoming what we're capable of. You must stay dedicated and driven always to widen your lens and push your limits beyond what's comfortable. Stop letting yourself settle into the comfort and complacency of where you are now. You have to acknowledge and show up as the person you're intended to be—despite the hurt, the insecurities, the failures, the fears, and the challenges you've had to face. These are the roads you've had to travel, and it's all part of adapting, growing, and developing you and your story. How you show up and who you become on that journey is entirely up to you.

The Gateway

This is your moment of decision. If you want to crawl back into your hole and settle for a subpar life, then shut this book right now. I developed this book for those who are ready, willing, and hungry for greatness and refuse to take the easy roads that will lead right back to their suck. I have also provided a resources page with additional tools to assist you. When you define and acknowledge exactly what your suck looks like, you can then run from it and chase down your lighthouse. Never allow yourself to settle back into the subpar life that too many accept for themselves. You are built for greatness, and that can only be reached by expecting more from yourself, creating a mission to never take any movement that leads to your suck, and doing the work to ensure you uncover the potential within you.

At this point, you have allowed yourself to settle for living within your brokenness, hurt, damage, fears, and arrogance for too long. You need to take the time to fix how you view yourself. The fundamental principles in this book will help walk you through the process that will "open your lens" and allow you to see a new vision of who you are and who you can become. You cannot let your lack of knowledge and direction be the holdback that keeps you from identifying your greatest asset, which is you. Work through the process I will cover in these pages and build the foundation for your best future.

The opportunity for greatness is in front of you, and you can take it on, chase it down, and push forward despite any hardships, difficulties, or issues you may have faced or currently be facing. Many of you have limiting beliefs or lack drive and ambition, which will be the cause of your acceptance of a lesser version of *you*. Your suck keeps pulling you back into your comfort and the path of ease rather than the hard road. You choose the simplicity of the known rather than the adventure of the unknown. To understand all the ways you are drawn to your complacency, distractions, or other holdbacks rather than taking life head-on and chasing your best future, you have to define your suck.

As you work through and develop the best version of you that can show up, you need to detail and document specifically what your suck looks like for you and differentiate the ways the two different versions of you show up. Clearly define and choose which of those versions you will allow to be the driver toward your future. You are at a catalyst point in your life; you can choose to settle for the easy roads, or you can chase the future that you know you're capable of having. The road you are called to travel requires you to show up driven and dedicated each and every day.

What will your life look like? Will you be left with regrets and failures because you didn't take the required steps and work through the process? The roadmap is right in front of you, and your suck can finally be behind you if you execute the plans developed throughout this book. You have a decision to make—live in your suck, or suck less and do better every day as you move toward who you are built to be and what you are here to achieve.

CHAPTER 2

Your Lens Is Broken

My eyes opened to flashes of lights as they wheeled me through the hallway of the hospital. I had no idea how I got there. My last memory was trying to finish a one-mile run around a local lake. Frustration flooded my thoughts. I knew it had happened again—my heart had given out, and I had been transported to the hospital. After living a life full of achievements and setting records for my physical abilities during my law enforcement career, I became reliant on my physical performance to feel successful. During my career as a police officer, I was in a terrible car accident. I was "T-boned" in the driver's door and paralyzed for months as a result.

To make matters worse, I was then diagnosed with the onset of a major heart condition. That was the end of my journey as a police officer and the start of a major uphill battle. I struggled to accept my physical limitations and the fact that I was no longer able to perform as I once had. I became depressed and felt like a failure. I tried the "mind over matter" approach but knew that my heart condition wasn't going away and urgent transport to the hospital would eventually happen.

Being wheeled through the hospital without any memory of how I got there was a huge smack in the face and another knock to my pride. The doctors explained to me that my heart had stopped, the EMTs had to revive me on the scene, and I needed to take my situation more seriously.

Unfortunately, I had been transported to this hospital a few times under similar circumstances and hadn't listened to the warnings from these professionals. My life as a high performer was over, or at least that's what I thought. I had to make a change, or I was going to end up dead on a path somewhere or in a serious medical condition where recovery was not an option.

I struggled to make sense of why this had happened to me. During this time, I fell into a depression and pushed away all the people who were close to me. I felt like I was no longer good enough and that everything I had done was a waste. I was never going to be the same and would never be the physical "machine" I once was. The dark times that followed led me through a journey of discovery. Why was my definition of success tied to my physical abilities? There were so many aspects of who I was, so why did it matter that I couldn't compete like I once could? Why did I feel so worthless, insecure, unlovable, and useless? The answer, I learned, was that my lens was broken.

My childhood was filled with lots of great memories. I had loving parents, and they encouraged me in so many ways. They never set expectations for me as to what success would look like, aside from always having a great work ethic and staying dedicated to what I committed to doing. There were no crazy requirements of specific colleges or glorified careers they pushed me toward. But even though my parents were amazing people, they couldn't be everywhere at all times.

My older brother was a major tormentor during my childhood. He was always the bigger, stronger, and better-looking of the kids—and he made it known. As far back as I can remember, he mocked me for being overweight and weak, and he took every opportunity to prove his physical strength and ability to overpower me and beat me down. The fear of him coursed through my mind day after day, and I was afraid to tell my parents because I knew he would only crank up the heat. I was living in a competition with him that I did not sign up for, and I was destined to lose every single day. This part of my childhood shattered my lens. Back then, I felt that the only way I could feel good about myself and be accepted was to lose weight, become stronger, and push myself to compete with someone older, bigger, and much stronger than I could ever be. It was definitely a setup for psychological failure at some point in my life, but I had no idea my physical abilities would be stripped from me and that I would be facing a major mental battle at the age of twenty-three.

It took many years and ultimately finding a successful path in business for me to realize how much of a mental mess I really was. I was achieving results that other entrepreneurs and people within my industry would be ecstatic over, but I felt no excitement for my achievements. I set even greater goals for myself, pushed myself harder, and added more aggressive expectations to my checklist. I knew I had a broken lens and needed to rewire how my brain connected achievement to success to remove the requirement of physical performance.

I tell you this story to help you understand how a part of our journey will change our lenses. There are so many factors that will create cracks in our lenses. We need to be aware of this so we can know how to determine our expectations for who we can become. In so many situations, we find ourselves trying to look through these lenses to see ourselves as we really are, but they are so broken that we can't see the greatness we are or are built to become.

Going after your success and achieving your goals requires you to become aware and work through the holdbacks you face. The fact that your lens is cracked, broken, or even shattered means that the reality you allow yourself to believe may not be accurate and a major holdback toward your future success. *New York Times* best-selling author Shawn Achor touches on this by saying, "It's not necessarily the reality that shapes us, but the lens through which your brain views the world that shapes your reality. And if we can change the lens, not only can we change your happiness, we can change every single educational and business outcome at the same time." The vantage point from which you see yourself—your lens—has been skewed by the life you've lived and the difficulties you've encountered. You might be living in arrogance to overcompensate for your deep hurt or making less of yourself.

Just know that it doesn't matter how you cope with the issues. They are still there and will keep you from becoming who you are built to be if you don't acknowledge them and work to overcome them.

There are four main lenses that can be major holdbacks in the lives of so many people. In the clients I work with, and even in my own life, there are apparent issues from one, if not all, of these lenses and barriers on the road to success because of them. The four lenses are:

- the lens of you
- the lens of money and success
- the lens of your future
- the lens of your grind

Your life situation might not resonate with all of these, but I found as I worked through my life that there are cracks or fractures in all of these lenses. I acknowledged that I needed to do work in each of these areas to reach my full potential, and this is now required of you. Ignoring or refusing to see and identify your lens issues will limit your focus and success, and it will impact your future level of greatness.

This part of the book is intense, and some of you will try to disconnect and maybe even skip over it. I challenge you to push through this chapter with an open mind and a willingness to see which of these issues exist in your life. I have to address many angles and aspects of where lens issues can stem from, but it's unlikely to have all of them apply to your life. Understand that we don't know that some of our lens issues are even there until we open our eyes and learn about the different areas they can stem from. If for no other reason, read this to be able to help others you meet on your journey, as this will allow you to be more aware of holdbacks that can be present in each of us.

The Lens of You

Look at your life and the way you view yourself. The reality is that your lens is filled with cracks and fractures. For some, it may even be completely broken. You may not see yourself as you really are. You may not see your strengths, capabilities, abilities, and skill sets. Many different factors have impacted the way you look at yourself throughout your life. You are seeing yourself through the hurt and trauma you've experienced, what people have said or how they treated you, and your past failures and perceived inadequacies. All of the past relationships and difficulties you have faced and some of the things you've had to do to survive affect your lens. Each of us has a past riddled with unfortunate mistakes, troubling issues, poor decisions, and crazy hardships. All of these are a part of your journey, but none define who you are.

As you continue to work through your development and growth as an individual, it's important to understand that the lens through which you view yourself has these flaws. Your past is chock-full of lens-shaping and lens-cracking experiences. They start at a young age, and you must connect to some of the core issues from your family, your childhood, and your life in general. The early days of your life set the stage for who you are and who you will become, and that time has a considerable impact on how we look at ourselves. These developmental years significantly affect how we see our future and especially how we see ourselves.

The vantage point of what we see as our greatest potential to become is developed through and by the relationships closest to us, especially during our childhood. These relationships mold our ability to accept risk and influence the way we take on certain life challenges and struggles. These affect the pull to comfort versus the acceptance of the unknown. Our childhood brings limitations or expansion of how you envision your full abilities and the expectations that you place upon yourself to achieve greatness. Yes, there is a lot of greatness that can come out of your childhood. There is a lot of direction and guidance that can come through your early stages of life, but even the best of childhoods leave each of us riddled with different angles and issues that can create holdbacks in our process.

Even the best of parents have made mistakes and have issues that can create problems in the lenses of their children. I tell my son all the time that there's no handbook for dealing with the different circumstances I'm working with. I express that I'm trying my best, but I know that I make mistakes and am not the perfect father. Yes, there are a lot of parenting books, but there's no playbook that gives the answers to every unique situation you may face. You have to react and take action on the spot, which, even for the best parents, leaves a lot of room for mistakes and errors. Even wonderful childhood experiences with great parents still create issues and lens problems that need to be addressed.

You must also acknowledge the fact that your mother and father had parents who didn't necessarily handle everything properly. The compounding issues that are found over the generational handoff to each parental team (biological or not) connect deeply with your risk tolerances, ideologies, religion, money, business, education, and many other factors. This is found not just in the discipline and how they correct your behavior as a child, but also in the way that they provide guidance. There's a lot of verbalization of the limiting beliefs that held them back or catered to their comfort, risk tolerances, security and definition of success. Some parents have great expectations and specific direction that they give you, and others let their own failures affect what they teach you or try to correct their own shortcomings through you. Some parents provide excellent guidance, but others, consciously or unconsciously, might influence their children to not even attempt to define their greatness.

Some parents set specific expectations for you. It could be a college they think you should go to or a career path they think you should follow. They may push their definition of success on you or their view on what your future should look like. Other parents' belief systems might cause their children to limit their risks and take the road of security. Often, these expectations that come into play can cause limiting beliefs, create cracked lenses, and influence you to show up and make decisions based upon their lives, not yours. Most parents and adults come at this from a protective or caring nature, but it can create fear of failure and fear of risk, as well as an internal battle when your beliefs contradict the guidance of those you were taught to listen to.

Parents mean well when they set expectations, but it can sometimes be a major holdback when you are driving hard toward becoming great. You might be called to take risks beyond your parents' comfort. You might have to take a chance at failing that the prior generation would not have taken. Remember that you are called to become the best version of yourself, not the best version of them. They are not living your life. Consider all the instruction, advice, and childhood lessons—but never allow them to hold you back from your success.

You have to be willing to take on your own challenges, make your own decisions, and follow your dreams. This road can lead to hurt, disapproval from others, discomfort in relationships, and an upstream battle you must mentally work through to break away from the cracks in your lens. Your future is built on who *you* are and not their feelings or holdbacks.

When I originally had an in-depth conversation with my father—whom I respect and who is extremely wise—about my plans for launching my first business in 2008, his advice was to focus on finding a career or a job with a pension or retirement program available. In this area, his life and decisions were based on a mindset for security and the best route to retirement with that safeguard. There is nothing wrong with his opinions or belief systems about this. Still, I wanted to take the entrepreneurial road and chase this more unconventional path hard, understanding that it had risks. I appreciated his guidance and understood his concerns, but I had to run on my own road and live my life. I knew that if I didn't, I would be completely unsettled.

His mindset and his advice all came from a great place, but there's also the potential of a limiting mindset because of the way he was raised, his background or his greatest concerns. If I listened solely to that and accepted his beliefs, I would have never been able to look at my life through the right lens to determine the greatness I could achieve and the risks I was willing to take. His guidance didn't go unheard, and throughout my entire entrepreneurial journey, I have focused heavily on retirement investing and building my savings. Even though I didn't follow his original advice of taking a more secure path, I focused on his concern and utilized his wisdom to leverage a different version of it in my life.

You must be careful when dealing with family members, parents, siblings, and people in influential roles. There is a protective nature involved, but many times the voices of other people become so ingrained that you adjust your lenses, and in some cases, that can be crippling to your future. You cannot lose sight of your potential future because of these protective mentalities, mindsets, or other cracked lenses that the people around you hand off. You must take a step back and identify what aspects could come from other people's protective nature and other parental figures' mindsets rather than based on who you are and what you are built to become and achieve.

To make sure I'm covering all the major issues and ruffling all the feathers, I have to address situations where there were overprotective parents who created a significant lack of resilience, situations where you were coddled and protected to an extreme so that you never had to face the struggles and difficulties that life brings. Your family, parents, and others around you—who always protected you from the harsh reality of life—did you a major disservice. It created a lack of resilience and drive, the absence of a hunger for success, and a lack of motivation to strive for a better future. It stripped you of the ability to get out of your own way.

These cracked lenses can create a deep-rooted issue where you might expect somebody else to fix the problem, work through every step with you, and walk you through to some sort of success where you can feel you have achieved something. Your life is right now. It's right in front of you. Nobody else can or should take ownership of your road except for you. You need to look at your cracked lenses and determine whether you came from a situation where you were enabled, overprotected, or overprovided. Identify what life is calling you to become and in what areas of your life you will have to focus greater action. Your situation might not be as extreme as the picture I painted above. Still, if there are any elements of this in your life, even minimal, they need to be addressed and cut out immediately if you want to discover what you can become.

As I mentioned in my intro story to this chapter, and as I've seen throughout my life and so many other people's lives, siblings can be another factor in creating cracks and fractures. In some situations, your lens might even be demolished. Sibling rivalry is real and can create an environment where you compete for attention and approval, which can significantly influence how we see ourselves. The competition always seems to be rigged for them to win and is almost always based on their strengths. They spin things in a way that makes them feel great but lowers the people around them. Some siblings can be relentless, unforgiving, mocking, and bullying—all activities that leave us broken. Sometimes, siblings take on the protective or enabling role they have seen in their parents toward their brothers and sisters. You have to comb through your life and uncover every area where your lenses might be cracked or fractured and need to be adjusted.

To those who had parents who took it too far and created an unsafe environment for their childhood, I first want to say that I'm sorry that was the road you had to travel, and there are no excuses for their actions. Second, I want to tell you that your excuses need to stop. Stop living in the past. Don't let it define you. Yes, you have been impacted by abuse, whether verbal or physical, and it doesn't matter if it was from your parents, siblings, or someone else—it can cause major damage to your long-term lens of yourself and how you view what you're capable of. The hurt and difficulty you faced is nothing to ignore or shove deep into your hurt basement, but you have to acknowledge the issues that could show up in your life because of it and then push forward to overcome your trauma.

Don't let the abusers continue to control your life. Working through your lens issues and overcoming them will become a part of your story and your journey to greatness. Don't use these issues as excuses when you fail or reasons why you don't succeed. Identify now where the cracks in your lens are coming from and then charge hard in the opposite direction toward your success.

You have to comb through your life and determine what areas have cracked your lens and are keeping you from seeing you for who you are. Your true abilities and what you can become will always be held back by the lenses you're looking at yourself through unless you do the work required to overcome. The fractures or cracks in your lenses make it difficult to see your potential. Your future requires you to break free and connect to the core issues in your lenses to accept your strengths, connect to who you are meant to become, and drive hard into what you are built to achieve.

The Lens of Money and Success

Success and money are defined early in our lives before we even understand it. Being raised in the family group you came from and spending time around others formed, fractured, and cracked your money and success lens at an early age. It may sound ridiculous, but I have seen this firsthand, working with countless entrepreneurs. They make decisions and move in a direction based upon ingrained wiring deep within them. I've seen families live paycheck to paycheck and borrow money from their 401(k) each and every year despite their high annual earnings. I saw some of these families go from earning $250,000 in a year to $650,000, and the issues remained, even without buying a new house or car, just by completely wasting money. The deep-rooted wiring of money and success can be devastating when it comes to your future and your long-term financial freedom.

I'm constantly seeing the connection between cracked lenses and the inability to gain momentum toward financial freedom, asset retention, and true wealth. Some people hold onto a false reality that money is bad or that life is more difficult with more money. Sometimes, there are impacts from things seen or heard in the family, in church, or during childhood that frame your mindset on money and future success. Some people encourage utilizing government systems rather than achieving their own success or financial freedom. Other families communicate expectations of less-than-stellar outcomes, normalizing poverty and economic difficulties to their children from a young age. It's a major problem when parents make excuses to their children for their lack of drive and ambition and their financial failures because that teaches their children not to work to feel better about themselves. The effects of all of these examples can be destructive to your financial future and success. You have to work backward, from the present through the past, to identify what you have heard, seen, or experienced regarding money and success early in your life that created a crack or fracture in your lens.

There can also be guilt for being successful or wanting financial freedom. You might have difficulty because you watched your parents struggle financially as you grew up, and you have a deep-seated feeling that you don't think it's right or okay to gain wealth or success. Seeing people that you know and care for not achieving the same results or lifestyle can be mentally crushing and a holdback in the process, but you have to understand that you can only be responsible for your own hunger levels, your own drive, your own ambitions, and your own actions.

You can't take risks for other people, and you can't pull people out of their comfort zones and make them take on the challenges you are willing to take on. You are called to develop the best version of yourself, and you should be dedicated to that and never have any reservations about achieving your greatness and success and building wealth. The people around you are moving to the beat of their own drum and may not be willing to take on the challenges that you do. You should never underperform to make others feel comfortable or satisfied with their actions and results. You need to get hungry, find stupid amounts of success, and influence other people along your journey.

Is money the answer? Absolutely not. You can be filthy rich and still be stuck in your suck. Money is a tool, not an outcome. It brings experience, stability, and specific lifestyles. But when you use it toward your suck, it will all be useless. The tool needs to be directed and in the hands of the right craftsman. Some people have a lens that glorifies money as if it will fix all their issues or is the end goal. Singer and songwriter Bob Marley puts it in a straightforward and clear way: "Money is numbers, and numbers never end. If it takes money to be happy, your search for happiness will never end." Chasing money alone will leave you empty unless you understand that it's merely something to be leveraged to help you fulfill your greater purpose or get you to your end goals.

As you continue through this book, I will help you dig deep into your driving forces to make sure that you can really find success throughout the process and not just find yourself miserable and unfulfilled with money in your bank and numbers on the page of your net worth calculator. Please understand that I'm not saying money is evil or telling you not to chase it. I just want to help you understand that money should be a part of your goals, not the end goal. Money is part of the journey and a tool you can use, but it's not the *purpose* of the journey. It's okay to want money—it's actually great for this to be a part of your desired outcome—but be cautious of making this your sole purpose and desired outcome.

Your drive, hunger, ambition, and want are all part of the fuel that propels you forward. You want greatness, you want results, you want wealth, you want success, and you want a better future, so never settle. The more you achieve, the more opportunities you will have, and then it's up to you to handle those opportunities wisely and determine what you will do with them. Never apologize for your results, never apologize for your success, and never shy away from your greatness. It's time for you to step up and chase after your success by removing any mental barriers that are the cracks in your lens about money and success.

The Lens of Your Future

The lens of your future has been limited by all of the issues we've already gone over and so many more that are potentially there from your past, your childhood, and your experiences. So, as you chase down your future, you need to focus on it through the lens of potential and unlimited success. It's great to dream and to go after lofty goals. Why settle when you are called to find your greatest results? Stop looking at your future through your rearview mirror and focus on what you see through the windshield. Achieving greatness and becoming the best future version of yourself will require discomfort, growth, and development, and it will necessitate inspection of the lens through which you have been looking at yourself and your life. Your greatest achievements are still in front of you, and your ability to see yourself and your future through the actual lens of who you are and what you are capable of is a part of this catalyst in your life.

The holdbacks in our lives can stem from many different places, but the lens with which you look at your future needs clarity and potential. Every one of us—yes, this includes you—has issues holding us back from seeing our full capabilities and potential. The future you will build for yourself requires you to take a step back and examine the lens through which you are viewing your entire life. What are you built for? What does the greatest version of you have the ability to achieve? What do you want your future to be?

Asking yourself these questions and identifying your lens issues are part of your work in this journey. Touching on this in this chapter was an essential part of the reflection you will need to do on the lens issues in your life. Chapters 5 and 6 will push deeper into this and help you connect further with the lens of your future and the core elements needed. You might feel unscathed at this point, but I've been taking it easy on you. Uncovering your future potential and what you are built for takes much more than a small part of a chapter.

The Lens of Your Grind

To some, the term "grind" might have a negative meaning, but to those same people, the work required to find success is a deterrent that's holding them back. Dedication to the process is what those people lack, and major future success is what they will fail to achieve. The grind is nothing but positive when you know why you're grinding and the outcome you're chasing. Think about what you do with coffee beans before you put them into an espresso machine—you have to grind them. It's part of the process that turns them from beans to a magical cup of deliciousness. So, why is the term grind such a negative thing? The grind is just a step in the process toward a better outcome. The same is true for your life—the grind is just a part of your progress toward success and a better future. The grind is not the suck. Instead, it is your escape from your suck.

Each and every day should build momentum out of the suck and toward your lighthouse. This will require daily sacrifice, focus, and acknowledgment of the broken lenses you may have. You must be ready to do the work needed to grow, develop, and even repair the cracked lenses. True success is only found through the process of the grind. Your life will only be as great as the hard work and dedication with which you approach each day. A daily focus and a daily grind to suck less and do better every day is necessary for your future success.

You are blessed with the ability to take on the grind, and it will be the proving ground for your grit and determination. This will be the gateway to unlocking your future success through the learning, strengthening and evolution of who you can become. The decision to run from your suck is the easy part—staying focused on your lighthouse and putting in the daily grind to suck less and do better is where those who will succeed and those who accept failure will part ways. Your daily efforts toward your goals, toward your future success, and your lighthouse are wasted if you allow yourself to go back to your suck. Living your life focused on your future, identifying growth, seeing your development, and hitting the milestones on the way to your success will give you the momentum to push through the grind. Having the right mindset will keep you connected to your purpose and prevent you from being derailed by the easy roads and comfortable paths.

Always remember that you are never finished developing yourself. You have the ability to continue to grow, better yourself, and grind toward your greatness. You cannot live in the vision you have of yourself through the cracked lenses—you need to continually work to overcome these obstacles.

The first step is to identify the cracked, fractured, or broken lenses and acknowledge that they exist. The second step is to determine the root causes of these issues. Be the inner two-year-old who keeps asking "why" until you get to the core of where things started, and then utilize your current, more mature vantage point to determine the reality of the root cause and the truths behind the beliefs. Eliminating the hardship and the holdbacks that are keeping you from seeing yourself for who you really are or what you are capable of achieving is a major part of this process. This might just be a daily acknowledgment that the past has no power over your present. For some, it might require working through this with a mental health team, and for others, creating daily recordings, posting notes on mirrors, or similar things will work to eliminate these negative mindsets. For you, this book might be part of your healing.

I hope that as I walk you through this journey and you connect with the core of who you are and what you are built for, you will see the greatest version of you that you can become. You cannot ignore your broken lenses. You can't allow them to hold you back. Instead, take control. Work to correct and fix your lenses to reach your full potential. The best and greatest version of you is waiting for you to take ownership of your life and become the author of your story.

CHAPTER 3

Write Your Story, Not Mine

From the moment that you opened your eyes and took your first breath your story began. The pages of your life story became flooded with progress, information, hardships and achievements. In the early part of your life, there were so many influences and adjustments to your story, some of which you felt you had no control over and were authored by people from your family unit. In many cases, authorship may have been spread out between many individuals. As you continue to grow, develop, and mature, authorship transfers from your family unit and the people around you into your own hands.

This process seems challenging and, in many cases, includes wild paths, crazy adventures and learning experiences that are a part of shaping your global story. There is a required turn in the writing process where you have to realize that you have full control over the authorship of your future and your story. To some, it comes early and they are eager to take the seat and write endlessly to make sure their story becomes the best version capable, and to others, they go through life making excuses and blaming others. The transition of ownership for the authorship of your life is handed off to you whether you are ready or not, and no one is left to blame for what occurs in the rest of your story but you. Your life cannot be full of excuses from your past and other's mismanagement of their part in your story. You have to connect with the reality that your story and outcome is only yours to write.

The amazing part about being the author of your own life is that you can adjust the way circumstances are viewed, handled, and expressed. You recognize that there are third parties still trying to influence your story and that life circumstances will occur, and your story must be written to include these difficulties. However, your story does not end in those moments, hardships, or challenges—they are just chapters, small parts of the entire adventure of your life. Some people might blame others, make excuses, and act like somebody else controls their story. I agree that some parts are influenced by others and by crazy, unexpected turns that are out of our control, but it still holds true that it's up to us to create our outcome. *It's up to you to navigate the obstacles and the difficulties and constantly drive toward success despite all odds against you.* The best stories, movies, and inspiring real-life accounts always have major hardships followed by great triumphs. Why would your story be any different?

Many people wallow in their difficulties, hardships, obstacles, and hurt and wish that they could live somebody else's story instead. The hard reality is that you have only one shot at writing a story, and that story is your own. The comparison game, the "it's not fair" game, the "but you don't understand" game, and any other mental games that make excuses for your lack of ownership are devastating to your story, not anyone else's. When you take a deep dive into other people's stories, you will quickly find that even though the challenges they faced are different, the hurt and hardships are deep-rooted and require grit and determination to overcome. You have to focus deeply and push hard to change the course and direction of what appears to be a disaster, hardship, or series of obstacles. There is no getting out, there is no escaping, and there is no switching stories—the only way is through. Figure out how you will bring the difficult parts of your story together to create a climax that will never be forgotten. When you are in the middle of a storm, you have to decide how to write the recovery and the rebuild. Your focus must be on the outcome you're chasing rather than soaking in each chapter's specific hardships or challenges.

As you begin to focus on the fact that it's important for you to write your story and not mine, it is vital to understand that the "mine" I'm discussing is not me, not my life, not my story, but rather a replaceable placemark. This is for you to enter anyone that you are jealous of or envious of their circumstances. Enter those you feel have an easy road, those who have lives you want, or those you put on a pedestal. You cannot look at them from the outside and state that you wish you had their life when all you see is the best parts of their stories. Stories are not built from the climax but rather through the journey of how they got to their peak. You need to see what it took for them to reach this level and gain their results. Who someone is will not be defined by the high points of their lives. Who they are is found through the journey—by conquering their hardships, taking life's challenges by the horns, and turning them into greatness. If you take an honest look at the lives of people who are at what you may consider their peak, their road has been scattered with difficulties. Their grit and determination to overcome is how they became the person capable of achieving greatness and worthy of all they have achieved.

There is both a calming and scary realization that comes with knowing you only have one story to write in your life. You can't escape your story. It's time to take ownership of it and write it with your long-term goals and successes in mind. Navigate through each turn, hardship, and obstacle. Take on your life head-on and create a story that you are excited to be living. Be relentless during the hard times, humble during triumphs, and always hungry for the best version of yourself to show up each and every day.

Turn Envy Into Admiration

As you sit back, connecting with the fact that you are the author of your story and working on plans for your future, it's important to understand that no story is exempt from hardships and difficulties. Dwayne "The Rock" Johnson, Tony Robbins, Steve Jobs, Oprah Winfrey, Sylvester Stallone, Stephen King, Tom Cruise, Walt Disney, Albert Einstein, and Michael Jordan—all of them pushed to achieve their greatness despite the roadblocks and hardships they faced. Their stories were written through their dedication, hunger, ambition, and relentless drive to never settle and keep moving forward despite anything they faced.

They all had a lighthouse they set in place for themselves as a clear vision of where they wanted to go and who they wanted to become. They pushed forward without excuses and without giving in to the difficulties. They refused to fall back into comforts, simplicity, and complacency. Each and every one of them had rejections, failures, and internal battles they had to face, but they never quit, nor did they let their fears and insecurities win. Instead, they have lived a life with a suck-less-do-better mentality, always showing up as their best version and chasing hard after the most remarkable success they were built to achieve, always charging toward their lighthouse. Minister and activist Dr. Martin Luther King, Jr. stated, "The ultimate measure of a man is not where he stands in moments of convenience and comfort, but where he stands at times of challenge and controversy."

The stories of others who have pushed past their hardships and difficulties to become great should be terrific encouragement for whatever situation you are facing and whatever part of your story you have to write yourself through. Now you know that your life's difficulties and hardships have given you the ability to write the part where you overcome and conquer all odds. Why do you feel that your life should be any different from all these others who have had to overcome incredible odds and difficulties to find their success? They never settled into complacency or comfort or gave in to their fears. They were constantly pushing hard after their goals for their future and showing up daily to find their greatest success. *The rewards don't come without the work. The struggle is what provides the strength.*

Strength Through the Struggle

You are not exempt from this standard formula of life and the required development of who you can become. There will be hardships and difficulties, but the more complicated the challenges you face and conquer, the stronger you will become and the sweeter the success will feel. If you want to fly, you have to strengthen your wings. When I was in Costa Rica touring a butterfly garden, I watched as the butterflies struggled to exit their cocoon. The guide explained that you should never help a butterfly exit its cocoon because struggling is part of what prepares that butterfly's wings to be ready for flying. If you assist, the butterfly won't be able to survive because it will not have the strength to fly. The same thing is true in your life. *A part of what you're preparing for in your future can only be achieved through the struggles and hardships that you are called to face now.*

I often think that God must be trying to make me into a beautiful butterfly—well, maybe not beautiful. It seems He's constantly throwing hardships and difficulties at me, which are challenges created for me to overcome. As I face these obstacles, it's encouraging to know that I'm being strengthened for what He has in store for my future. It is 100 percent up to me how I show up each day, interpret the lessons I learn from each situation, and grow through the process.

Similarly, the best version of you will show up only when you have fought through your hardships, learned to stomach the grit of the hard times, and have become relentless at pushing hard at your future success despite the obstacles in your road. If you have nothing to overcome in your life, how can you tell the story of climbing the crazy mountain of your life? I am constantly looking at my life, the hardships I've been called to face, the difficulties I've been through, and the mountains I've been called to climb. I won't give you a false narrative—during many of these challenges, I asked, *Why me?* I went through a season of being mad at God. I almost lost hope in some of my darkest times. But thinking about these times allows me to see the strength

I've been able to gather and the hardships that I now know I can take head-on. Whether it be medical problems, financial problems, relationship problems, mental health problems, or anything else that I face in my life, I know I can overcome them because of what I've been able to see myself working through.

In your life, if you have nothing to overcome, how can you really become great? You will only rise to the level of the obstacles and challenges that you are faced with. The deeper that you have to dig to conquer the hardships in front of you, the more capable you will be to unlock your best future. The easy roads produce the weak and the complacent person, but the hard roads are for the relentless and those who have proven they are able to overcome and succeed. The best version of you will only become known and rise by taking life head-on and setting your goals higher. Require yourself to achieve greatness. Fight through all the difficulties to achieve the best version of yourself.

Facing Your Life Head-On

Major holdbacks keep you from writing your story and achieving the outcomes you strive for. Acknowledge these holdbacks, face their existence, and take daily action to overcome them. For some, their fears are their holdback. For others, constantly wishing for other people's lives is the holdback. And then you have those who hide behind excuses for their pain and their past. The situation you are in today is not what defines you—it's what you do with the future in front of you and how you overcome your mindsets, holdbacks, and fears that make you the person you want to become.

Maybe your life is riddled with fears that are keeping you crippled and pushing you toward comfort and complacency. Fears are not only a potential holdback but also contribute to derailing your decision-making, which can push you away from showing up as your best version. I know in my own life, there are a few fears that I wrestle with on a daily basis: rejection, failure, and a nagging feeling that no matter what I do, it will not be good enough. If I had let these take hold in my life, I would never have launched my first business, never taken on my first employee, never put anything out on social media, and never built my businesses to their level. There is no way I would have written this book because it is way outside my comfort zone. But I wasn't willing to let my fears be the holdback in my life and keep me from the lighthouse I'd been chasing. The same can be true in your life.

Complete honesty with yourself is required, and you must be prepared to be fully open to discovering where your fears are sitting in your life. It's important to acknowledge the fact that you have these fears and that they will cripple your future success. Take inventory of your fears and uncover your crushing mindsets so that you can conquer and overcome them. You need to know where these fears are stemming from. Does your fear come from the situations or circumstances when your lenses were cracked? You need to work back to the root cause to fully understand and connect with the weight of the fear in your life. Take hold of those fears, acknowledge where they come from, and work through each and every one of them so that you can take action despite their existence.

I encourage you to start taking charge of your own life and be the author of your future. Each story of greatness is riddled with challenges, difficulties, and hardships. Stop wanting to live a life that's a mix-up of everyone else's highlight reel, best moments or successful outcomes. Stop focusing on the lives of others and choose to focus on the authorship of your own story. Create a lighthouse and a future for yourself, but shut out the noise of other people's lives and base it upon who you are.

The narrative will look completely different when you start wanting to design your own life, become dedicated to bettering your future, and strive to achieve the fullest version of what it can be. Drill down to write a story that you will want to look back on and read. Stop living in a way that is destined to bring you regret over missed opportunities. Stop wishing for other people's lives, and instead, go after a future based upon who you are and what you are built to become.

Embrace the Authorship of Your Own Life

You are the author of your story. Nobody else is writing it now but you. Take ownership of yourself each and every day to achieve the success you know you're capable of. Stop giving power to those who have created hurt or placed holdbacks, fears, and roadblocks in your path. You have to regain control of the authorship of your life and realize that no one else is going to write the story for you. Rather than creating a vision board based on other people's lives, you should connect the reality of what you are built for and how you want your story to be told.

Take a moment to answer the following questions to reflect on this process:
- Are you, right now, the best version of yourself that your story will portray?
- Are you done bettering yourself?
- Are you done improving on the person you will show up as?
- Is this the best version of yourself that you are capable of?
- Have you unlocked your full potential?
- Are you telling me that you cannot become a greater version of the person you are right now?
- You can't show up for your family, career, business, financials, or God in any better way than you are now?

These questions should get your mind racing on ways you can show up to write your story differently than you've allowed it to be written up until now. You have to set your goals, target, and mission and identify what it will take from you to achieve that success.

In my life, I have identified the fact that I will constantly work to better myself in every possible way. I am never going to settle for complacency in any area of my life. I know I want to become *great*, so why would I ever settle for just being *good*? The crazy part is that my definition of great is a constantly moving target. Some might say that's an unhealthy aspect of who I am, but I find that it has become one of the things that drives me and pushes me each and every day. Knowing that no matter what I achieve, I can always work to better myself and find a more incredible version of success, impact, love, and knowledge.

It's part of what keeps me humble, hungry, and dedicated to suck less and do better each day. I know that I can always learn and grow to push myself to become even better than the version of who I was yesterday. Ultimately, it doesn't matter what difficulties or hardships you're facing. You are the author of your story, and you have to take ownership of each aspect of your life. Every day that you have in front of you should be an opportunity to determine what you want your life to become. And after that, you have to chase hard after that outcome.

Your story isn't over as long as you have breath in your lungs. What will your story say? What do you want the end result to look like? What do you want to be known for? Will your story be an inspiration to others, or will it just be another story full of complacency, comfort, and somebody whining about the difficulties they faced? Once you've determined your story, you have to decide what you're going to do with it. Are you going to allow your life to become just another comfort-zone-chasing, weakness-accepting, fear-crumbling, and insecurity-empowering life? Or will you write a story that will provide encouragement, inspiration, and an example of a relentless dedication to a greater future?

As you live the current version of your story, look at each day as an opportunity to change the course of the entire climax and outcome. Acknowledge your position as the author, and determine what the next pages of your story are going to say. Dig deep and identify what is making you hungry to become better and achieve success in your future. Why do you want a greater story than the current one you are living? Why do you want to overcome your obstacles and prove that you will never quit? Why do you want to become great and achieve success? In your life, as the author of your story, what are the driving forces pushing you to write the story about the unstoppable version of you?

CHAPTER 4

Ignite Your Driving Forces

I sorted through the seemingly endless stack of paper in front of me and felt my blood pressure increasing and my ears turning red from the stress. The calculator had added more digits than I had imagined as I totaled up the bills, debt, and the mountain of expenses I was facing. I compared the bank balance and what was estimated to be coming in over the next two months and knew that financial failure was imminent. I worked through every angle and spent countless hours grinding on this process but finally had to force myself to stop and try to sleep, knowing I had a giant to conquer in the coming months. This moment was eight months after taking a huge risk and starting my first business to chase my dreams. *Had I made the wrong decision? Were they right when they said I would fail? What had I missed? What did I need to learn?*

I had just gotten married, my wife had lost her job, and I had just signed the papers to become the father of my wife's daughter. I had taken on the responsibility of being the provider but felt I was failing as a dad, husband, entrepreneur, Christian, and man. I'd worked through every angle possible and was struggling to see the light at the end of this tunnel. As I trudged through these days of mental stress, I was trying to work through the options at hand, realizing I had limited time to determine my next steps as bankruptcy was a growing risk. An opportunity presented itself as a perfect solution—a six-figure job opportunity that could solve all of the financial issues I faced.

This sat deep in the pit of my stomach because it would mean I would have to walk away from my dream of building my business and achieving the success I had set out for. As days passed, I came to realize that the anxiety of taking this easy way out and walking away from my goals would not just be a major failure for myself but would also cripple my hunger, drive, and ambition, along with my desire to prove to my family, friends, and those around me that overcoming obstacles is something we're all capable of. I now had to wrestle with the choice of taking the easy road or continuing down the obstacle-filled path and focusing on fulfilling my why.

I took days to work through this inner battle and had to mentally step back to connect with the reason why I started this journey in the first place. I went back to the goals that I had set, the purpose for taking this leap, and the deep-rooted reasons for choosing this hard road. I had to determine whether I was ready to continue facing the risk to hopefully gain the potential reward or fall into comfort and security. The decision became more evident as I realized I would never be satisfied and confident in this new job opportunity, as I would have to let part of myself die to accept the offer. If I took the job, I would fail in achieving my goals, destroy my driving forces, and kill the dreams of who I knew I could become. I had conflicting emotions as I pulled my phone out and called the company's CEO to decline the job offer. How could I feel crippling fear and relief all at the same moment? I knew I had made the right decision, but I had to go back to that stack of bills, dig deep, and put a plan in place to avoid filing for bankruptcy—and then drive hard toward my comeback story.

The next few weeks were full of planning and digging deep to draw on every ounce of encouragement, fuel, and ambition left inside me. I knew I had to run toward my goals, the better version of myself, future success, and the desired outcome I was after. I had to take inventory of all my abilities, knowledge, experience, and business foundation—everything I had available to move the business forward faster—and figure out how to scale. This moment was the catalyst for my entire future, and the only way to ensure success was to push hard into my driving forces and focus on my *why* to ensure I never allowed myself to doubt my direction again.

There are moments in your life when you find yourself at a crossroads and in the midst of hardships, adversity, extreme obstacles, and perhaps even an easy way out. These critical moments define who you are and who you will become. The fuel you need should come from the core of who you are and the driving forces that cannot be turned off. Surface-level reasons will fade, goals for monetary gain are short-lived, and you need to determine what factors ignite your hunger, fuel your passion, and turn you into an unstoppable force. Keep digging until you know the root cause for each of your driving forces so you can fully understand what keeps you moving during the hard times. It's easy to chase money, wealth, attention, security, and respect, but you must connect with your deepest driving forces and determine the foundation behind your why.

Restless, Unsettled, and Relentless

Your restlessness and drive to discover a better future are fueled by an inner hunger and a more profound purpose. Take inventory of every push you felt, every spark to your flame, and every fuel for your fire. It can appear in different areas of your life and be a part of your driving force in many ways. Detail out the areas of your life where these feelings originate or reside, and connect to the root cause of the *why* that keeps you moving each day toward a better future.

Many people run through life always hungry, running after new results without a clearly defined purpose. This keeps them constantly chasing an outcome based on their feelings rather than the root causes. You need to determine why you're restless, not settled, and what makes you a machine dedicated to a better future despite the hard roads. You have an inner drive that keeps you moving forward when others give up or take the easy road. You are built differently—laced with hunger, a burning desire, and a restlessness that doesn't allow you to just fall into and accept the average goals, outcomes, successes, and life that other people have. What is it in you that won't let you settle? Where is this coming from, and what is its purpose?

The reality for you and me is that we have these relentless driving forces that need to be understood and channeled. Does the relentlessness come from goals for your future, your finances, and what you can become? You need to discover and understand your why and your driving forces so that you can learn to channel this, especially during the hard times and the challenging roads. Driving forces are very specific to each person and can stem from many places in our lives. Your life and motivating factors are vital because you can use them as fuel during your journey and your daily grind.

In choosing to continue on what seemed to be an impossible road in my life, I had to take inventory of every potential driving force to use it as fuel to overcome any obstacles. I will tell you that it took every ounce of fuel in my tank to keep me pushing through all the hard times I faced after I made this tough decision. Some people make light of chasing their dreams and give up every time they face hardship, but I'm not built like that. I am relentless and have learned to channel all the fuel I can gather to keep pushing despite any circumstances. Your situation is no different. You may not even know all the hardships you will face as you move down this road to achieve your greatness, but I guarantee you will have extreme ones that will test your relentlessness. Take inventory and channel everything you can. Have it ready as fuel for those moments when you find yourself about to give up and take the easy road.

Driven Toward Your Goals

Being goal-oriented is an incredible way to maintain motivation and keep a long-term focus. Goals are vital to channeling our efforts and concentrating on the long-term output. These goals are our compass for our dedication to our mission and keep us focused toward the end result. Being driven toward and having long-term dedicated goals in mind is absolutely vital for so many of us, but we have to be careful about what the goals are and where we are focused. As a goal-oriented person, you often create a checklist of goals, successes, and achievements that become your primary focus. As you start achieving these goals, some leave you feeling empty and needing more fulfillment. As a goal-oriented person myself, I have created checklists for successes that I once thought would fulfill me, but I've learned that money in the bank won't fix the pain, the fast cars won't take away the hurt or the past trauma, the business success or the awards won't quench the thirst or the hunger for the real future I am called to and the success I am built for. Financial freedom, extravagant trips, and flashy jewelry will not fill the void where your hunger comes from or calm the push that leaves you constantly unsettled.

Let's talk for a minute about the material things I just mentioned. I am not saying that they aren't fun things to have as a part of your goals. I love fast cars—the more cylinders, the better. I know some of you like the twin-turbo life, and I get it. To me, though, there's nothing like hearing a V10 scream as you wind it out. Traveling is another thing that money can bring, and I love experiencing it with my family and having the freedom that comes with financial success. What I'm trying to say here is that your goals should never be limited, and your driving forces should be more than wealth and fast cars. The goals you set need to be a part of the success that will make you satisfied with who you become and what you've accomplished. Setting goals and driving toward goals that are created without understanding your deepest-rooted driving forces will only leave you empty at the end of your achievements. Having a driving force to achieve your goals is not enough. You must connect with the why behind each goal to determine whether they will get you to the level of success your inner self will be satisfied with.

While going through the process of uncovering the *why* behind the goals you're setting, work through some of the following serious questions:
- Why are these goals important to you?
- What is the purpose behind each of the goals you're setting?

- What will accomplishing your goals do for you?
- Why are these goals there in the first place?
- What is the core driver for each of your goals?
- What are the feelings you hope to experience when you accomplish these goals?
- What is the problem these goals will ultimately solve for you?

Take the time to connect with the rudimentary aspects of each of your goals and determine the real driving forces behind them. Without connecting to the core of each one, the satisfaction you will receive upon completion or achievement of the goals will lack the potency to really quench the thirst behind them. Gaining the connection to the driver for each one unlocks the fuel that will make you unstoppable once you determine your true lighthouse. You will then be able to create a checklist that will allow you to achieve the goals that will get you to the greatest level of success and make you feel fully accomplished.

Fear of Failure

Fear is often associated with creating a lack of action, but to many, the fear of failure is used as a part of the driving force in their life. It's part of what is pushing them forward and giving them a relentless spirit to never give up. The channeling of this fear into fuel can be a great tool as long as it doesn't include massive side effects that are actually holdbacks because of what the fear stems from. When you delve into the cause of your fear of failure, you might discover that there are specific people, moments, or other direct factors that have made this a major fuel in your life. These same factors could also be a part of the broken lenses we've discussed and might have other major effects on your life. You have to connect with the specific fear inside you and focus on identifying its root to determine what other side effects could be coming from it.

Learning to properly channel fear as fuel and determine your definition of both failure and success is vital. Having an undefined global definition of failure will not always push you toward success. Instead, it can be a major distractor and something that will keep you moving back toward comfort. A lack of action in your own life is one way to guarantee failure. Executive coach and motivational speaker Ryan Leak states, "What's worse: failing while trying or failing by not trying?" One thing I know from my own life and others I have worked with in this area is that it becomes difficult to determine who sets the bar for failure in our lives and who is the defining voice of success. If you fail to define these factors clearly, frustration may build up because you're chasing a moving target. Until you connect, identify, and define these, your life can be a constant psychological rat race.

The one thing that holds true is the fact that action is a must, and your life requires momentum toward your goals and ambitions. Define what failure and success will be for you based on your life. If you don't, there could be a swift transition from using the fear of failure as fuel to it being the cause of your burnout, thus ending your relentless drive toward success.

As you push hard and take on risks to hit a level of success in your life, there will be times when you need to recognize that things aren't going to go as planned. This is where you must define the experience as a learning opportunity rather than a failure. Hard times don't mean you're failing—they're opportunities to learn, develop, and adapt. Adapting is never failure but rather proof of resilience and the ability to overcome obstacles. This is where defining failure and identifying the lens issues that might derail your progress is both important and required.

To many, failure could be defined as giving up on your journey and achieving less than greatness because you chose to take the easy road. For myself, I am constantly pushing to better my life and who I am, and I'm always working to clearly identify my lighthouse and then move forward every day toward that lighthouse. So, failure to me is accepting less than greatness on any one day and then not requiring myself to rebound and recover the next day. I am dedicated to moving into and through each day with a mindset and a purpose to chase after my long-term goals and not allow myself to get sidetracked.

Failure for me includes allowing myself to be derailed by holdbacks, fears and insecurities, and the distraction of shiny objects. You have to take the time to define what failure looks like in your life and your exact situation. Fear of failure as a tool used at the correct times to drive you in the right direction can be an incredible asset, but leaving it undefined can be extremely crippling and even a major holdback in your life.

Insecurities and Fears

Channeling insecurities and fears in your life to use as fuel for your future can be leveraged in a positive way, but if not kept within proper bounds, it can be a part of your burnout and derailment. It's up to you to decide what to do with them. The danger comes when you're not willing to identify and accept the insecurities and fears in your life. How can you leverage what you're not willing to acknowledge and face? Everyone has to deal with insecurities and fears, but how that looks can vary. Some people counter their fears by disappearing silently into the shadows, while others might become loud and boisterous and even appear to be overconfident and egotistical. You can cater to your fears and let them win or push to conquer them. For example, if someone is insecure about their knowledge base and feels they are inadequate for the opportunities they want for their future, they can give up and change their goals, or they can work to build their knowledge base each and every day. The faster you work to acknowledge your fears and insecurities, the greater your ability to filter and focus the output.

When channeled properly, feelings of inadequacy can be the driving force and motivation you need to learn and develop. However, caution is necessary to ensure that these challenges don't become demons from your past that might hinder your progress toward your goals and your lighthouse.

You don't want to settle into those negative feelings and emotions. Instead, let them encourage your growth and push you to overcome your obstacles.

For example, if you were raised in a low-income family and you're trying to change the course of your life to escape the poverty you lived in, you may be insecure about your roots and where you came from. But you use that as a driving force to prove that you can achieve greatness despite the assumed outcome that is expected from people raised where and how you were raised. I spoke to one entrepreneur who was raised in a low-income area locally, a neighborhood with drugs and gang violence. Very few find success after being born and raised in this area. After discussing his upbringing with me, he proudly told me that he was able to shed the shackles he had from being born and raised in that "godforsaken area." He said that overcoming the mental obstacle of having to say that he was born in that area was a major hurdle he had to get past. This became a part of his driving force to achieve such a level of success that no one would even think twice about where he was raised. He focused on achieving greatness that would inspire others and be a true story of triumph.

My family had no entrepreneurs, and no one had gone into business for themselves. I was taking on an unknown realm, and I had a lot of insecurities and fears that I would not be equipped to succeed. I used this as fuel to chase after every opportunity to learn, grow, develop, and educate myself. I went to school for business with a specialty in accounting and earned my bachelor's and master's degrees, which I felt was just the tip of the iceberg as far as the knowledge I needed. I dug hard into every business and leadership book related to the future I was chasing. I was, and still am, in a constant state of development and growth, and I am grateful for the insecurity that was once present in my life and my ability to channel it as fuel.

Each one of us has insecurities that we face about our past, our upbringing, where we came from, or certain situations we had to overcome. Many times, there are things to be proud of when you look back at what you've had to overcome through the process and what you've achieved despite the odds against you. Some of these insecurities need to be carefully reviewed on occasion because although they might be pushing you in the right direction and helping you overcome your obstacles and chase down your goals at the moment, if untamed, they could keep you in your comfort zone and be holdbacks that keeps you from becoming the best version of yourself.

Similar to insecurities, we all face some type of fear in our journey. Your struggle could be fear of rejection, the unknown, judgment, or taking action. To some, it may even be the fear of becoming like someone else, someone who failed their family or caused issues by their lack of action, complacency, laziness, or failure to provide. The fears that run deep inside of you can surface in so many different areas of your life. You might be burdened by a fear of going through a similar situation you've already been through, or the fear of allowing yourself to fall into complacency or comfort, or the fear of not reaching your full potential and failing yourself, or the fear of allowing yourself to settle for less than what you're built for.

I will openly admit that I have many fears, and some of them are listed above, but I know that the thing I am terrified of is not becoming the version of me that I was called to become. As the sign in my office says, "I will not settle on good. I am called to be *great*." I work to take daily action, fueled by my fears, toward the greatness that I know I was built to become despite my fears.

You don't have to allow your fears to cripple you, hold you back, and be a barrier to your success. You can choose to use them as fuel to constantly better yourself. Taking inventory of your fears is absolutely vital so that you understand the roadblocks you might hit and be aware of the crippling effect each of them could have. This inventory and acknowledgment is a part of your checks and balances to make sure you don't allow yourself to fall back into comfort versus driving forward despite the fears.

Life will pull you away from your future greatness if you don't identify your fears, insecurities, and doubts and take them head-on. Could they be major holdbacks in your life? Of course, but you need to make them a part of your why and your driving force. Once you do that, you can take on your future, conquer the complacent and insecure version of yourself, and achieve the greatness you desire.

Money and Wealth

Money is one of the most commonly used driving forces as it is very surface-level and easy to connect with. You, like many, might have this glorified idea of money and how great your life will become once you have it. Yes, money is a great tool and can maximize your experiences, security, lifestyle, and so much more. Money will get you the attention you might want and some really cool stuff, but chasing money alone will not be enough to get you the real success you're chasing. Successful entrepreneur Gary Vaynerchuk said, "When you chase money, you're going to lose. You're just going to. Even if you get the money, you're not going to be happy." You need to think about why you're chasing money. What are the core driving factors that are pushing you? Why is money your biggest driving force? What will the attention you get do for you? What are you trying to solve in your life by chasing this goal?

Money itself does not bring the success you want and will not give you fulfillment. Right now, your lenses might be limited, and you might believe that money is the solution to all your problems and will satisfy your hunger and drive, but you will quickly find that there are deeper-rooted factors at hand. Those I have seen chase money as their primary focus have found themselves making bad financial decisions. They have a momentary financial success, then fall back to once again struggling financially. Money is a tool that, in the hands of those with a deeper purpose and drive, can be used to reach further greatness, but it will be a major stumbling block for those who have only a surface-level connection to their deep-rooted why.

Let me help you connect to this further, using my life as an example. Money was a part of my driving force, but the root was security for my kids.

I was riddled with medical issues, and with doctors telling me at one point that I had a shortened lifespan, my goal was to achieve financial security for my family before I died. So, was money a part of my driving force? Of course, but it wasn't the core driving force. My family's financial security was.

Some people chase after money to get the attention they want, but fast cars, flashy clothes, and expensive jewelry aren't the driving force. When you dig deep into this, what is the true core driver? Is it acceptance? Countering fears? Do you want money for the people in your life? Or is it to prove that you can overcome obstacles? The deeper roots of the hunger for money and wealth are almost always driven by many other factors that you need to push into and connect with to channel as part of the fuel that keeps you moving forward.

The Who Behind the Drive

The most highly successful people I have met and worked with all have a major driving force based upon specific people or God in their lives. When you review stories of successful people, you will find a common theme of being driven and motivated by the people around them. As I have expressed, in my own life, money was not the driving force—the real driver was my kids and bringing security to my family. Is providing a better life and future for your family your driving force? Are you driven to be an example to those around you to prove that anything is possible? Are you driven to be a leader and a guide, living to lay the groundwork for others to follow? Are you trying to give back based on what someone has done for you? Did you have a role model growing up and strive to follow in those footsteps?

This last one hits close to home in my life. My father was a killer example of always growing, developing, chasing, and being dedicated to bettering himself and working hard despite his challenges. I remember early mornings when I was growing up. No matter what time I woke up, my dad was already up studying, learning, growing, and bettering himself. He was focused on his future and providing for our family. I am always pushing hard to show that his example was not in vain. His dedication is a constant driver in my life to continuously develop and better myself.

In your life, some people need you to show up as the best version of yourself so you can provide security or a better future. Some people come to America to provide a better future for their families. Others dedicate themselves to earning multi-generational wealth to stop the cycle of poverty for their loved ones. As you take inventory of your life, push deep to find the core drivers that move you forward. Consider what you want to accomplish or overcome for your family or those around you. Making an impact on the people in your family and those around you is one of the greatest driving forces you can channel toward achieving your end goal. This will keep you dedicated to your journey and ensures that you have the fuel required to overcome obstacles that you will face.

Your Inner Voice or God

It's the inner voice telling you that you are built for more, the one that will never let you settle and is always driving you to push harder. You know you're capable of so much more than you're showing up as right now, and that voice drives you to always discover a greater version of who you are. Our inner voices might be different, but yours (and mine) are calling you to show up bigger, better, and greater. To some, this inner voice is God, calling you to take specific actions and wanting you to make the most of the talents and abilities He's entrusted you with. Wherever your inner voice comes from, it's driving you and pushing you toward a specific calling and helping you connect with the fact that you are called to be a leader, set an example, and have an impact on those around you—and it all starts with you increasing your abilities, skills, knowledge, and clarity every day.

Help Build Connections

You might find yourself lacking close connections or core relationships and are hungry to build connections with others and be a part of the business or entrepreneur community. There may have been times when you felt like an outcast, but now you feel like success and money will help you be accepted by others. You feel like the you that you're striving to become will allow for more opportunities to build relationships. The desire to be a part of a community, build relationships, and find acceptance from others can be a hard-charging driving force in your life. It just requires working through the hurt, uncovering the truths within you, and being honest about the fire brewing inside of you. Use it all as fuel for your future.

Help Others Overcome

It is a raw truth that your life has brought you hardships and difficulties throughout your journey. You may be driven and motivated by the fact that you will have the ability to help others overcome similar circumstances after you find your way and conquer these struggles in your life. You might hunger to help others who are going through hard times or needing answers. Your life experiences might drive you to want to be the light for others, to be a guiding force and show them what they're capable of, and to help them understand that this is nothing but a temporary obstacle in their path. Your driving force to be a part of other people's hopes, changes, and journeys to success can push you to find new greatness, help you stay dedicated to your process, and overcome any roadblocks on the road to your lighthouse.

Proving the Enemy Wrong

The dedication to growth and the requirement to find all the potential driving forces in your life lead you to push past your comfort zone. To make sure there are no rocks unturned, we need to discuss the reality that there are people in our past who have created pain, hardships, or even trauma in our lives. A part of our driving force might be proving them wrong by overcoming the circumstances or issues they said we would not be able to overcome or hitting the levels of success they said we would not be able to achieve. This enemy mindset and proving others wrong can be great fuel to get you moving and keep you from falling back into your complacency, but you have to acknowledge that there are limitations to the extent and sustainability of this power.

The fact that you have this pain and these issues from your past is something to acknowledge, connect with, and understand how to leverage. You may always have this goal to prove others wrong, but it will not be enough to get you to the full, unstoppable version of who you are capable of being. There are many things to consider and layers to unravel to understand this driving force inside you.

What were the others really saying, and what does it mean in your life? Were things said directly, or was it indirectly through jokes, actions, and the way it made you feel? In some cases, you heard some brutal and destructive things that created deep hurt and even major adjustments to your inner voice. You may have heard things similar to what I heard, "You'll never be good enough," "You're going to fail," or "You're dumb, fat, stupid, lazy, useless." The pain from the words "I hate you," "I wish you were never here," "You are a mistake," and "No one wanted you" is a definite hurt from those moments in time. They are now ingrained in our minds and often said to inflict a wound out of anger or spite, especially when delivered by people we care about. The scar tissue is there in each of us, but what you do with it is up to you. You have the ability to turn this into starter fuel to push you hard toward the actions required to achieve your success.

There are some counterbalances that you have to be cautious of and avoid focusing too hard on. You must be careful about how much weight you place on others' definitions of success or being good enough. These might not be what you are built for and might not be based upon the greatest success you can achieve. They have their definitions, and you need to create your own and stop allowing your future to be driven based on their statements, criticism, and deep-rooted issues. Running your life focused on their definition and statements could very quickly put you on a path that's not intended for you. Your mindset needs to move past these moments, hurts and pain. Base your mindset on what you are intended to become, not on others' expectations or what they claim you will never be able to reach. This can be the starter fuel that gets you to take initial action, but it will burn out, and then what? You must have a greater goal and definitions of what your greatness looks like and what you are built to become.

Let's touch for a second on the sustainability of this as your main driving force. Considering what they said to you, what is good enough? What is success? What is showing effort? What is stupid? What is useless? What is a failure? What is being a loser? What is the bar by which they were judging you? There was no specific definition for any of these. They were meant to hurt you, and many even lacked any truth. So why allow yourself to churn over them? Are you going to constantly chase after an undefined counter to their statements? Are you trying to fix past hurts by your future actions and results without having any clarity about the statements that were made? If this is just about outperforming specific people, is that your full potential? If it's just about proving these people wrong with an undefined measurement of the desired outcome, what proof will you have that you've proven them wrong? If you focus on this for your entire life, you'll be filled with negativity and constantly living in your past versus running toward your future.

You never want to limit your potential satisfaction, growth, and long-term happiness by always having to focus on the negativity from others from your past. You need to set your guidepost and lighthouse of who you want to become based upon all of your driving forces, and then proving them wrong is just the icing on the cake. I'll be the first to admit that there are seasons when I have used this as a part of my fuel pack to get moving, get started, or keep going. I wasn't at the top of my class or voted most likely to succeed. During middle and high school, I was usually the butt of jokes and harassed, ridiculed, and picked on, so I understand the mental struggles that come with this territory.

Even when I became a cop, I was hazed rather extensively and was the standard subject of jokes because of my age, lack of life experience, and ambitions—it was relentless. These are the times you look back on and know you have scars, but they can't be the entire focus of your life. The core fuel for your life should not come from your darkest places or past tormentors. It should not come from the foundation of pain from your past. If this becomes your main driving force, then every day will be fueled by negativity, and at what point in your life will you be able to shut this off? It can serve as a starter fuel but should never be your long-term driver.

The driving forces that will get you to unstoppable success and lead you to become the best version of you need to come from the goals you set for your life. These should be way beyond the pain, hurt, and issues from your past and with the greatest version of you in mind. Your future should be more than just proving others wrong. Your why and your lighthouse must be specific to you and developed from your life, your situation, your deep-rooted hunger, your past, your pain, your fears, and who you are built to be. You need to know your motivators, your starter fuel, your dark places, and your long-term goals. They will keep you focused on reaching the greatest version of you. You cannot ignore these crushing pressures but channel them all into a driving force that will keep you pushing despite any obstacles you face. The suck you are charging away from needs to stay behind you, and fully grasping your driving forces will make sure you are charging forward, dedicated to your lighthouse.

CHAPTER 5

Hyperfocus on You

The room felt so small as all attention was turned on me. I was being questioned about why I was making the choices I had made and why I felt I was going to be able to start and build a business. My excitement was quickly extinguished as the doubts flowed in from those closest to me. Many of the comments were made out of love and concern in an attempt to protect me, but hard questions arose that made it impossible to stay focused on the planning and foundation I had done to make this decision. What started as an exciting announcement quickly turned into an embarrassing moment where some of the comments made me believe I had a false sense of reality. Had I completely missed the mark on who I was, what I was able to do, and my ability to chase my dreams?

I tried to defend my decision and my reasons for going in this direction, but the flood of questions and concerns began to cripple my drive, and fear began to settle in. Maybe my family and friends saw something I didn't. Maybe I was just chasing a pipe dream. Maybe they were right. Will I fail? Did I lose my mind? I had to go back and rethink everything to figure out what I had missed or why I even thought I was capable of this. Maybe I should take my dad's advice and find a job with a pension or retirement program. Should I be listening to all these comments, concerns, and doubts from others? What do I do with the hunger in me, the want for something more, the drive to find my greatest output possible? I fell into complete confusion, and all the clarity I had at the start of the day turned into scrambled eggs mixed with fears, insecurities, and doubts, topped with a bit of humiliation.

The drive home that night was a blur, followed by a restless night filled with thoughts that I had wasted too much time on this pipe dream and needed to snap out of my false reality. I needed to get my head straight and put a plan in place that would be a viable option for financial stability. The fears and insecurities crept in as I replayed all the things that were said and focused on each of them like they were wisdom from above. Who do I think I am? How could I be confident that I could take on such a huge challenge and actually succeed in business? How did I let myself believe this was going to work? What was I thinking?

Over the next few days, I worked back through all my planning and concepts and asked myself why I felt I was able to take on such a challenge. I went through my strategies, processes, and even the launch plan for the business. I dug deep into my strengths, weaknesses, capabilities, and developmental plans. Reviewing all of this groundwork and the planned risks and potential rewards, I came to terms with the fact that I wasn't crazy. Maybe a risk taker, but not crazy. I thought about all the comments I had heard and realized that many of them had come from those individuals' deep-rooted fears, low-risk tolerance, doubts, and protectiveness over me. These people loved me and cared about my life and my future. There had been no ill intent.

However, I could not live according to their feelings, beliefs, or concerns. I had to move forward with the challenge I knew I could take head-on and conquer. My parents had always demonstrated and expressed the importance of learning and growing to better yourself, and I knew I was built to go beyond the comfort and security of the norm. I had to live my life and allow others to live theirs. I had to hyperfocus on myself, my abilities, my skill sets, and my strengths.

These inner battles, feelings, and struggles, the constant juggling of who you are, what you want for your life, and the continuous noise that is everywhere about what others want, need, or expect can become a crushing weight that many people crumble under. Being pulled in more directions than you can comprehend becomes a crippling effect that will anchor you until you fail unless you get control over the situation. The expectations, opinions, concerns, and even pessimistic mindsets create a major distraction and can possibly derail your focus. This, coupled with your internal voice, fears, and insecurities, creates a constant challenge in determining the correct direction to take. You must be dedicated to cutting out the noise and focusing on you.

Take the time to hyperfocus on yourself and become clear about who you are, who you are built to be, what you are chasing, and how to become the greatest version of yourself. This sets the standard against which all external noise is measured and helps you to gauge the validity of others' information, expectations, or concerns.

Some of you have not really come to terms with who you are and your abilities, strengths, weaknesses, and negative cycles. The caution or concern from others should be considered, but it has to push you back to a greater understanding of yourself. Your drive should always be to grow and develop with the focus of understanding who you are. Cut out other people's opinions, fears, insecurities, and personal holdbacks. They are not the ones who are going to live your life. They are not writing your story.

My life would have been drastically different if I had not done the work to fully focus on myself and determine what I am built for. Knowledge of my skill sets, abilities, and strengths—as well as being aware of my weaknesses and my holdbacks—allowed me to detail the risk through my lens and make a decision to execute despite the concerns of others. The same is true for you. As you keep chasing success and pushing hard toward your goals, you have to be 100 percent real with yourself. Know how you work, where you thrive and the greatest skill sets you have. Be honest about your holdbacks and weaknesses so you're able to maintain your progress versus falling back into your suck. You are your best asset and the number one tool to get you to your greatest success.

As you read this chapter and work through the questions, it's vital that you remove the connection to your career, job, business, industry, or wherever you may be or have been deploying your efforts. This is about the core of you, not how you are currently leveraging or utilizing yourself. I have worked with many individuals, entrepreneurs, and business leaders who, through the process of fully understanding themselves, have come to realize that they are focusing their efforts in the wrong arena or direction. This is not about getting confirmation that you can gain some success within your current role, industry, or business. It's about connecting with who you really are and what you are meant to achieve.

Your Greatest Asset

You are currently living your life, adjusting your daily habits based upon where you think you should go, always lit by these fires, fuel, and driving forces that you've just uncovered in your life. The real question that needs to be answered is, do you have a realistic understanding of who you are and what you're built for? I'm not talking about surface-level but extensive discovery of your skill sets, abilities, personality strengths, brain processing, and the greatest areas of strengths that are your core abilities. So many people run through their lives and really don't have a total comprehension of what their strengths are. They are focused on feelings, emotions, opportunities, and luck to push them in the right direction and make decisions rather than really understanding who they are and how they are built to make sure they are putting their efforts into the areas that will get them the best results.

It's not a matter of being good enough, skilled enough, detailed enough, or focused enough. It comes down to using the right tool at the right moment for the right reason to get the right results. You need to look at yourself as the greatest asset in your life, really comprehend how to leverage your strengths, skill sets, and abilities, and understand your weaknesses to be able to utilize yourself as your greatest tool to achieve the success you're chasing.

Here's an example. Monster trucks are extremely powerful vehicles, but they could never keep up at a NASCAR race. Even though the average monster truck has about twice as much horsepower as a NASCAR racecar, they are built for a different purpose and wouldn't be able to compete. The same is true about you and how you are built. You have to make sure that you are the right vehicle for the race you're signing up for. As American novelist and icon Mark Twain said, "The two most important days in your life are the day you are born, and the day you find out why."

You want success. You are chasing your dreams. You are hungry for your results. If you haven't seen the theme here, it is you, so why would it be any different when it comes to your focus? You need to take this time to drill down into who you are, what you are built for, and the areas of yourself that can help you get the future success you want. You can't keep throwing your vehicle into any race with the right amount of prize money. This will leave you exhausted from failure and at the point of burnout, and you will stop trying to compete. The issue that leaves so many entrepreneurs at a dead end with so many past failures is the fact they never take a step back to fully understand who they are and then properly deploy their assets in the right direction.

Throughout my career working with entrepreneurs, I have had a front-row seat to those who succeed and those who fail. It has been an incredible journey providing guidance and direction to those who have failed and those who have thrived throughout their career and are always pushing to new levels of success. *The one common theme I have seen in those who have become highly successful is that they are very self-aware and connected to their skill sets and abilities and are willing to acknowledge their weaknesses.* Even the humility of those who have hit major failures often opens the door for me to guide them and open their eyes to these significant challenges. Those who have dug deep and connected to their core have come back more driven than ever and equipped to overcome obstacles and achieve their lighthouse.

Are You Real With Yourself?

In working through your life, how real are you with yourself about who you are and the areas of your life where you thrive and the areas where you falter? Have you connected to the importance of taking the time to reflect, learn, and grow to develop as the success machine you're capable of being? As you're working through this, you need to ask yourself if you're being honest with yourself or letting your arrogance get in the way of your growth and success. The lighthouse you're chasing, the success you're going after, and the finish line you are racing toward aren't places for your arrogance. Humility is the key to growth, and you must be ready to learn at every corner and from every issue, every relationship, every conversation, and every moment. Those who allow their arrogance to consume them will turn into a *rock* versus a *sponge*. A rock cannot absorb. It becomes complacent, unmoving, and stuck in its place. A sponge can take on and absorb, grow, expand, and adapt based on the climate around it.

I completely understand that confidence is a part of what makes you successful. But you have to make sure you have the foundation behind your confidence and understand the aspects of who you are and your abilities. I consider myself a confident person—I know who I am, and I am connected to my skill sets, abilities, and the core of what makes me successful—but I am also very aware of my weaknesses and the areas where I do not thrive. This gives me the knowledge I can leverage to engage with other people to help me perform in those areas. Maximize your greatest strengths and leverage the greatest strengths of others. Being confident means knowing your best skill sets, knowing your best abilities, and being satisfied with who you really are.

The process of connecting with and becoming confident in who you are requires taking a giant step back and really learning and knowing the core of you. I'm not talking about taking inventory—I'm good at this, I'm good at that. I'm talking about really going into an in-depth process of understanding yourself and your greatest aspects, as well as all the weaknesses and holdbacks.

To show up as the best version of yourself, you must be real about who you are. Your future, your goals, and everything you set in motion should always be based on what you are built to be and focused on the greatest version of what you can become.

Pay No Mind to Others' Voices

As you move through your life, it's very easy to get sidetracked by other people's voices, opinions, or expectations. Take some time to understand some of the ways that other people can influence you, and then remove their voices, their wants, and their expectations of you so you can focus on who you are and what you are driven to become. Other people's voices can become a crushing weight and a major distraction, and you must eliminate them from your journey.

From a young age, you might have been told who you need to become, what you need to be great at, or what you should do. Your life should not be driven by the expectations of others but should be a fulfillment of your goals and ambitions. Nowhere is there an allowance for other people's opinions to be a part of your mission, your life, and your future. Maybe there were expectations regarding the college you should attend, the career path you should or shouldn't pursue, or the amount of money you should make. Perhaps there are general expectations about work, ethics, or where to live. These expectations become ingrained in your psychological processing, but it's ultimately up to you to decide whether you'll allow them to dictate who you are now and who you'll become.

The challenge in this process is not just in identifying the expectations but also in dealing with the indirect comments and influences that may have been a part of your family dynamics from your early years. Your childhood years are formative and developmental, and what you see, hear, and feel during these early years affects your decision-making as an adult. The opinions, mental processes, and direction you choose throughout your life can be greatly influenced by things you heard and saw when you were young. Your risk tolerances are developed in those formative years, and you have to fight to push past them to accept greater risk.

The same people who put expectations on you had expectations placed on them as a child, and they don't always know how to stop the cycle. In many cases, they don't even know that it's even an issue. The faster you can remove these expectations and accept that you will make decisions in your life that others will not approve of, the faster you will be able to make clearer decisions about who you are built and driven to be. Your childhood was just another learning experience, and you now have to use your adult wisdom to identify what to accept as fact and what to compartmentalize as expectation and opinion.

The people around you don't feel the same calling, hunger, drive, and ambition that is inside you. They don't have to live your life, walk your road, and be accountable for your actions. They won't have to look back at your life and think, *Did I do enough? Did I show up in the way I was meant to?* If you follow others' expectations of you, many times, it's not going to fit your skill sets, abilities, and goals, and most importantly, it won't get you to your desired outcome. This will be the route to finding yourself stuck in your suck. I have worked with countless entrepreneurs whose parents have forced them to attend law school, medical school, music school, and almost every other school available. These individuals were not built for those careers, but the parents' dreams and expectations led their kids to find themselves stuck rather than chasing their lighthouse. As a hungry, driven individual or entrepreneur, it is important to turn off the noise from those around you, dig deep into who you are, and focus on your driving forces and desired outcomes.

Insight From the Few

In your life, there may be some around you who have great insights into your abilities, your skill sets, and even your habits or issues. Measure what you hear against the standards that you are setting in this process, which is based on the details of who you are and what you expect from yourself. Be cautious of the insight that you take from those you allow to remain as advisers in your life and keep true to the core of who you are. Those you take advice from should first be ready to hear about the process you have been through, the skill sets and strengths you have uncovered, and the lighthouse you have set for yourself. Be wary of advice from those who do not fully understand the life you are striving to live, and always stay connected with the person you are built to become.

In my own life and in the story I opened this chapter with, I listened to my family's concerns and feedback. I took it all in and compared it to all the work I had done to understand who I was and what I was built for. I had taken the time to fully understand my strengths and skill sets as well as the goals I was going after. Looking back, if I had walked my dad through everything I had gone through to fully understand myself and my goals, our conversation would likely have gone differently. Also, I should have known that my siblings would have snarky comments to make that would create doubt in me. They should never have been part of the circle I consulted about my direction. Without the foundation I had built in understanding who I was and the confidence I had created in what I was built to be, I would never have taken the next step down the path of launching my business after this conversation with my family. However, after looking back through everything I had done to prepare and still choosing to move forward, I was able to move with even more confidence. I had to be true to what I knew of myself, to the process I had been through, to my capabilities, and to the goals and driving forces I had put in place.

Guidance from others can be a welcome gift as long as it is based upon who you are, what you are built for, and the lighthouse you are trying to achieve. Don't limit your sources of insight to those who harbor preconceived ideas or expectations of you. It's crucial to ensure that the advice you receive is centered on your life and circumstances rather than influenced by their perspectives, low-risk tolerances, or desired outcomes. As you listen to others, you always have to take what they say with an ounce of caution and use your ability to decipher the information before putting it into action or practical application. Those you choose to take advice from should provide direction and guidance after understanding who you are, what you are built for, and the lighthouse you are chasing.

Who Are You Really?

Connecting to the core of who you are and uncovering the different aspects of what you are built for sometimes gets blurry. Your current role, business, title, and position do not define who you are but are just an output of some of your skills and abilities. These represent temporary adaptations of your capabilities, adjustments made based on the immediate needs of the moment or stage of life. The issue is that many people stop connecting with their core selves. They lose sight of who they really are and find themselves living as the person who fits into these molds. Through this process, you have to mentally disconnect yourself from your current role or position and allow yourself to unlock who you really are.

While having the right level of drive, ambition, and dedication is crucial, achieving the best results often hinges on learning to focus your attention on your finest skill sets and abilities. You are your greatest asset and your best tool, and you must fully understand how to utilize, maximize, and develop yourself. This is why Chapter 5 is here, where you need to hyperfocus on yourself. How can you set your long-term goals if you haven't taken the time to fully understand your capabilities? Your future and the goals that you set for yourself will be limited until you connect fully with your best asset—you.

When I was a cop, I was working day in and day out, living what I thought was a great version of me, but through those years, I had this inner hunger and drive, and I felt like I was not living to my fullest potential. Was I a great cop? Yes, I was great at chasing bad guys, great at hooking and booking and going hands-on with some good old-fashioned fisticuffs. The other cops around me knew I was a force to be reckoned with. They knew that if I were backing them up, I would never think twice about getting physical to incapacitate the threat.

At this stage of my life, I got some serious enjoyment out of being a police officer. I thoroughly enjoyed the adrenaline surges during some pretty gnarly emergency calls. It was a great time with a lot of amazing stories and experiences, but even while I was running hard in that career, I knew that my life was called to an even greater purpose. I didn't know what it was at the time, but I knew I had to start to dig deep and figure out who I was and what I was capable of.

At that point in my life, I was left to work through and identify a process to figure out what my life could look like and what capabilities I actually had. I knew that I was not going to be settled just by finding a new job—I wanted to see what I would be best at. The hunger continued to grow as I spent multiple years digging deep and trying to figure things out. I was a hungry, motivated young punk who couldn't really see my lighthouse and didn't know what my full capabilities were because I first had to understand who I was. I started taking personality test after personality test. Then, I dug deep into the career test, which led me down a path of curiosity about cognitive tests and mental processing tests. I signed up for every free test I could find, and every time I got results, I would read through them to determine who I really was, how I was built, and what I would be good at.

Through this process, knowing that I had a hunger for an entrepreneurial road, I started researching what industry options could be scalable and could turn into a business. I compared the different industries and the skill sets needed to my capabilities, personality, and interests. I spent some time working through and setting goals that, at that point in my life, I considered out of reach but represented a long-term focus for me to strive to achieve. Throughout this journey, it was crucial to connect all the pieces to precisely determine which industry I would pursue, one that would take me beyond the realm of law enforcement. I wanted to find something I could hit and achieve what I saw as my lighthouse at the time.

This process helped me understand who I was, and through it, I was able to start preparing for the next leg of my journey. It was the key that unlocked the start of my road toward becoming an award-winning entrepreneur with multiple highly successful businesses and an eight-figure sale of a business I was the founder and CEO of. At that time, I had no clue I would retire from my first career as a cop at age twenty-three due to a critical heart problem. However, I was determined to never settle until I discovered my full potential. It was a journey of really hyperfocusing on who I really was. I also had to work through all the mental holdbacks and issues that I went over early in this chapter, things that, if I let them fester and build inside of me, I would have never taken the extreme actions that I took. This entire process has allowed me to fully connect with who I am and constantly develop and grow. The core of the success that I have found stems from really knowing who I am and building my future plans based on the greatest success I am built to achieve.

As you look at your current situation, take the time to fully connect with who you are. Really hyperfocus on you. This book provides the foundational elements necessary for success and guides you to overcoming many common obstacles, holdbacks, and issues many people face. More than just a recounting of personal success, it provides a comprehensive roadmap to help you avoid major pitfalls and challenges that I and others have encountered. While reading this book is a valuable step, it alone will not lead you to your ultimate success.

You need to take the time to study yourself and uncover who you really are by focusing your attention and time on taking the different personality tests, career tests, and cognitive tests. The resources page for this book has links to different tests that I strongly recommend. After you complete the tests, don't just look at the results, charts, and graphs—you need to do the work to research all the different details in each one of your results so you can start to understand the "why" behind who you are. This information should help you improve your ability to learn, grow, and develop.

While working through these tests and uncovering more details about your core, it's important to reflect on your life and connect with how these results came to be. Think back to the times in your life when you've had jobs, projects, or situations where you felt dialed in and thriving. Review your test results and identify what it was about those times that connected you to your strengths:

- What skill sets were you able to use?
- What activities did you thrive in within your job or career?
- What part of building and scaling a business are you succeeding at?
- Where in your life do you feel like your efforts and your actions get you the greatest results?
- What do you feel most fulfilled doing?
- Where do you thrive when your effort is pushed to its fullest extent?
- What situations do you think allow you to show up as the best version of yourself?
- What activities in your business or career make you feel most accomplished?

Connect all of these answers back to the results you received on the personality, career, and cognitive tests and determine the consistency and areas where you showed up as the best version of yourself.

The same is true for the times that you felt failure or extreme frustration, like you just couldn't keep doing the job or project:

- What about this was outside of your strengths and maybe even a weakness?
- Why was this project or situation a completely wrong pairing for who you are?
- What about it felt like a square peg in a round hole situation where you were just not the right fit?
- Where do you feel like you were falling short or failing in building and scaling a business?

Connect all these back to your test results to determine where and how you were outside your skill sets or what you were built for.

Working through these and really digging deep into who you are can be very time-consuming and even frustrating, but it was a huge part of the catalyst in my life. The foundation I built during this discovery phase of fully understanding myself is a massive part of how I have become as successful as I am. The same is true for your life—the better you understand who you are and what you are built for, the more focused you can be in taking actions that are actually going to give you momentum toward your success rather than leaving you feeling burned out in a rat race.

Once you connect with who you are and what you are built for, you can start making decisions about the career you select, the industries you enter, the businesses you launch, or the team you need to build. Some of you will look at the business or career you're in and realize that you are grinding down the wrong path and need to determine what adjustments have to be made.

This part of your journey might take you some time to work through. I understand the difficulty some of you are up against and the hardship that making changes in your life could cause. This is why I am providing additional resources for more support and direction.

> Scan the QR Code for a resources page.
> For those listening to this book, the website for those additional resources is www.SuckLessDoBetterBook.com/Resources

The 80/20 Impact Rule

To focus your attention further on getting the most momentum out of who you are, it's important to connect to what I call the 80/20 Impact Rule. You are in the process of becoming self-aware, detailing how you are built, and analyzing your range of abilities and skill sets. There needs to be a clear separation of the abilities that have the highest impact on moving you toward the goals you are setting for your future and your other skill sets. The focus in your life is to sort out who you are and what you are capable of and channel the top drivers in your life that will have the most impact on your future success.

You must separate these into two buckets—the 80 percent and the 20 percent. The top 20 percent of what you are capable of should be the areas that you feel you are thriving in and getting the most results from, the areas you feel move the needle the furthest. The other 80 percent are abilities and skills that you are capable of and may even be quite good at but do not provide the level of results toward your future that the 20 percent does. There is some truth to the belief that as you work to become the greatest version of yourself and get the most results toward your future, the 80 percent becomes a holdback and a distraction from having the most impact on your future. This is all about you getting the most results each day in your business, career, and life and leveraging who you are to gain momentum toward your success.

Taking inventory like this is not a one-time process. It's vital to work through all of this right now, but as you continue throughout your journey, you have to connect back to this concept and constantly review and separate into these two buckets. As you grow and develop, there will be things that were once in your 20 percent bucket that will need to be moved to your 80 percent bucket. Those who are hungry and driven are always adapting based on their circumstances and the goals they have for themselves, so this separation has to be a moving element and not a one-time project. Entrepreneurs who are built for success and are on the journey to discover their greatest success will find that operating in their 80 percent will become the burnout, the holdback, and part of their suck. There is a great need for you to live in your 20 percent to thrive each day, have the ability to impact each area of your life, and create momentum toward your lighthouse.

You cannot set your lighthouse and future goals until you truly understand your skill sets, your abilities, and the greatest version of who you are. The majority of people fail to connect with who they are in their journey toward success and find themselves deep in their suck, losing hope for the dreams and goals they once had. To prevent your life from following that same pattern, you must take the time to review the aspects covered in this chapter and do the hard work to uncover your deep-rooted holdbacks and your true capabilities. Your lighthouse and future success are counting on you to connect with the greatest asset you have available, which is you.

CHAPTER 6

Set Your Lighthouse

She stared me in the eyes, and the words that exited her mouth created instant discomfort. She smirked and then took a bite of her dessert in an attempted seductive way, and I knew there was no way I would go any further on this first date. I was in a situation where I needed an exit. Sitting across from a 6'2" Brazilian woman who just told me that after dinner, she was going to take me to her house and tie me to her bed left me rather unsettled. This might have been a turn-on to some, but I am only about 5' 9.5" (I can't forget the half) and about one hundred and eighty pounds. She was not only taller than me but also larger in general. With my background as a cop, the thought of being tied to a bed by a woman I barely knew was concerning enough, but the massive size difference added a major element of danger. I quickly texted my babysitter and told her to call me in two minutes and tell me that there was an emergency with the kids. I was able to pay the tab and escape. At that point, I went back through the process of how I ended up on that date and made adjustments to be sure I got more clarification about the type of woman I would go on dates with in the future. I didn't think I had to ask a question about tying people to beds on the first date, but I guess I was wrong.

This funny moment was part of the journey I found myself on in my mid-thirties. My life had taken a crazy turn when I became a single dad after some very unfortunate circumstances. During this time, I looked back at the major difficulties laced throughout the prior ten years. There were many times of hardship and despair. I was constantly working on myself throughout these years and always striving to show up as the best version of myself, but it was not enough. I made my fair share of mistakes, but I worked to improve who I was. As I was reflecting on this period of time, I knew I could never go back to this type of situation again. I knew I had to do something drastically different during this dating process to get different results. I had to create a lighthouse for who I wanted to be with, the type of person who would be the right fit for the kind of marriage I knew I needed.

I worked long and hard to walk through all the hardships, difficulties, and issues in the marriage I had just come out of and determine what problems I could have contributed to versus the ones that were clearly not within my control. Digging deep into the complex reality of how communication was nearly impossible and how not feeling loved left me feeling insecure, hurt, and alone, I created a detailed complaint book. I knew that if I didn't want to end up in another situation like that again, I needed to be aware of all the issues and concerns I had encountered.

After this process, I needed to come up with an example of what the right woman for me would look like, something to set as my goal and my lighthouse. I included love languages, communication styles, beliefs, ethics, goals in life, and much more. I then created a dating process to identify the right type of woman for me—red flags to look for, questions to ask, and steps to follow. I had very specific rules in place for myself, including a three-date rule. This rule was to keep me from chasing a connection rather than following the process. If I met someone who showed any signs of my red flags or dealbreakers, I wouldn't allow myself to go past the third date.

I set out on my dating journey with this process in place, which definitely had to be adjusted as I implemented it with actual women. The one aspect that became the standard and the primary guiding light was the fact that I had created my lighthouse, the definition of the right woman for me. Through the twists and turns, including many other funny stories, I allowed my lighthouse to guide my decisions. This was strictly to make sure I never fell into another toxic relationship and never again felt the severe pain and hardship that I had finally escaped from.

There were moments and times when it felt so right that I wanted to ignore my process and just go with the connection, and one time, I even ignored my three-date rule. This situation was with a woman with whom I had a great spark. Everything felt right, but there were some red flags and issues that I was pushing to the side.

After the third date, I told myself that this one was trouble and I shouldn't see her again, but when the invitation came to spend more time together, I had a hard time resisting. It was in the middle of our fifth date when some of the flags resurfaced, and I was shaken out of the connection. I sat there as she continued to talk and realized that if I stayed on this path with this woman, there would be issues, difficulties, and a relationship filled with similar destructive tendencies. I excused myself to the bathroom to reflect on all the notes on my phone about the process and the cautions and rules I had put in place for myself. I realized that the date had to end, and I had to say goodbye. I knew that I had to take action and do it swiftly without a long, drawn-out process where she could convince me otherwise. I left the bathroom with cash in hand, walked back to the table, and told her I had to leave. I explained that she was a great woman, just not the woman for me. No hugs, no kisses, no walking her to her car, just a quick explanation, a goodbye, and an "I'm sorry." This moment was proof to myself that I had done the work to determine the lighthouse, and I had set the process and the cautions, but I had to stay true to them and not detour despite how hard the moments and challenges may be.

The outcome of this entire process and my dating lighthouse was that I met my wife, an extraordinary woman who checks more than all of my boxes, fits all the needs for who I am, and is an absolute blessing to anyone around her. I would have never met her or might still be single if I hadn't set my lighthouse, clearly defined what it looked like, and created the process of how to get the right results—or better yet, not get the wrong results—in the crazy dating process. I know it doesn't sound very romantic, but there is a major truth behind it.

Your life is now a train moving swiftly down the tracks you are laying, but most of the time, you are moving too fast and barely putting down tracks in front of you. The reality that must be faced is that you will never arrive at your desired destination if you don't set your long-term goals, plan your required outcomes, and define the station for your train to reach. I call this "setting your lighthouse," the guiding light you need in your life to connect all the elements I've discussed and set long-term goals you can spend every day chasing and moving the needle toward. This lighthouse will keep you on the right track and helps you identify those moments when you are derailed and need to pull yourself back in.

Distractions will come, shiny objects will appear, and you will be tempted to start chasing opportunities and ideas. Sometimes, you might even want to give up, but your lighthouse must always be there for you to check everything against and keep you motivated and moving in the right direction.

The Groundwork Laid

Throughout this book, I've laid the foundation for determining your lighthouse—long-term goals, ambitions, and achievements that you're driving hard after. You've been faced with really understanding the suck that you are running from or currently living in. You've had to connect with the fact that your lens is cracked, and now know that these cracks cause you to struggle with seeing yourself for who you really are and seeing your potential. By acknowledging this, you have had to work through the different aspects of your own life and take ownership of your story because no one else is going to come in and rescue you. You've dug deep into the driving forces inside you and connected with the reason behind each one. You have determined why you are pushing so hard and why you are so hungry, driven, and motivated.

You have identified the forces that push you toward bettering yourself, growing, and achieving greatness. You've connected with the work you need to go through to understand who you are and what you're built for, and you've gotten clarity and an understanding of what makes you great.

It is your time to break away and get to the planning and the dreaming, setting the goals for your future, and going after the greatness you want to achieve. Determine the level of sacrifice and dedication you are willing to put in and lay out the goals you want to set for yourself. Your groundwork has been laid in the prior chapters and prepared you for putting your goals and long-term planning in place. Too many people start with their goals and take action without the proper foundation, only to find themselves failing over and over again in their lives. You have the opportunity to have all the foundation needed and the groundwork laid to set a lighthouse that you not only can achieve, but you are built to achieve.

Far Out and an Extreme Stretch

Remove your fears and limiting beliefs to find the freedom to identify what your future could really become with the greatest version of you showing up. Look at potential outcomes of your life that might seem crazy. Let yourself hope for a future that seems unachievable at this moment. As I was initially working to set my own lighthouse and goals after I went through these processes and laid this same groundwork, I was focused on a future that seemed unreachable at the time. I was thinking far outside my box and incorporating growth and financial success that seemed beyond the scope of my capabilities at that time, but I was driven and motivated to chase a better version of who I was. The goals and ambitions I had set as my lighthouse in my early twenties became my focus and dedication. I constantly progressed, grew, and developed at every step of the journey, and I began hitting the goals and seeing the results on the pathway toward my lighthouse.

This process made me realize that the original lighthouse I had set was limited compared to what I was capable of. The results I was achieving led me to expand my lens of the greatness I was capable of, and I redeveloped my lighthouse. To put it into perspective, the revenue growth I achieved in one year was bigger than the entire revenue goal for the business when I laid out my initial lighthouse.

The results throughout my whole life have blown away the original lighthouse I had set in place. Because of that, I have realized the importance of chasing hard after something greater than what you feel you can achieve in your current situation. *The lighthouse that you set should be what some may think is a little crazy or beyond your reach.* It's absolutely impactful to see how chasing your extreme lighthouse and growing and developing toward that end can change the outcome of your entire life.

At this point in your life, don't be timid or afraid of setting far-out goals for yourself—reach for the stars. Your lighthouse should not be achievable in your current moment or based on your current knowledge or capabilities. It must be based upon the potential that is reachable only through developing your best skills and abilities. Think about how much more you will be able to accomplish as you compound your growth and work through the process of bettering yourself. Your greatest version of you and your best work is still in front of you. If you focus on using your 20 percent and staying away from your 80 percent, chasing hard after bettering your life with hunger, drive, ambition, and fuel, what can you achieve?

Remember that this is about compounding the driving forces you have now connected with, removing your broken lenses, and getting a hyperfocused future to chase after. You are dedicated to connecting with the best version of yourself and focusing your efforts toward this lighthouse. These goals must be a stretch and way beyond where you are today to make sure you're always moving forward and becoming the best version of yourself. This approach will keep your movements and actions on track, moving toward your lighthouse and dedicated to the future that you are hungry to achieve.

You must live with a destination in mind and put in the effort to make you the machine that will never quit. Utilize the dragster approach, using all the power needed to push forward toward a core purpose rather than the pinball approach, with your efforts thrown all over the place. Be dedicated to the end result while building all the principles that you can repeat and adapt to any new track you decide to focus on based on the moment. The difference is knowing what you are built for and fully defining your lighthouse as your core mission. The lighthouse you set for yourself must be an ambitious stretch that requires learning, extreme growth, development, and adaptation.

Based on the Future You

The easy road will always lead back to your suck, but the hard and dedicated road, using your driving forces and best skill sets, will lead to your success and your lighthouse. To achieve a greater version of yourself and the success that you are built to achieve, your goals should be extremely uncomfortable and require you to become a better version of yourself than you are right now. Your lighthouse should be entirely out of your comfort zone, something you might even feel ridiculous putting in place. Just remember, you are never finished, and how you choose to live your life each day is a constant development of who you will become. *Never settle for a lesser version of yourself than you're capable of.*

Your future is a canvas that can be developed as you go, but you have to focus on the vision of what you want that canvas to look like in the end and then always move toward that vision. You are built for greatness, but you must develop your strengths and abilities, build on them, and deploy them on the right road. Each of us needs a lighthouse to make sure we're always building in the right direction. Too many entrepreneurs and hungry individuals settle for a lesser version of themselves and allow their complacency to surface due to fears, insecurities, or limiting beliefs. Your lighthouse must be based upon the greatest future version of you and what you can achieve.

Passion and Courage

Many people believe that passion and courage are enough to achieve your best life and the future that you are built for. Some say that this will lead to your greatest success. If you search this topic, you will find people on both sides of this opinion. The truth is that this is hard to prove or disprove. In some situations, passion and courage have lined up with an individual's abilities and skill sets and they have achieved great success. Then, there is the complete opposite, where people have the passion and courage but completely lack the abilities. I remember when *American Idol* first came out, and there were all the clips of the people who had passion and courage and were trying hard to become a singer, but it was clear to all of America that they didn't have the ability. If you never watched this, a five-minute Google search will give you some good laughs and an understanding of what I'm trying to explain here.

The other important aspect of passion is the fact that it often doesn't lead to a place that will be able to provide at the level you want or need financially. I have worked with many entrepreneurs who have chased their passions and failed miserably because they didn't consider whether their passions and the industries could provide the financial means to get them to their desired outcome. A part of setting your lighthouse should include your financial goals and desired income levels, both active and passive.

To connect you to a painful example, one of my clients came to me after he left his high-paying corporate job, making over half a million dollars a year, and was excited to tell me how he was following his passion into the health and wellness space. He launched a gym in the heart of Central Florida and almost immediately located a few other local failing gyms and merged those into his brand. He loved the ability to impact people's lives and was extremely passionate about people finding recovery through fitness and wellness.

The hard truth was that he had chased a passion and had the courage to take action, but he lacked the right plan. I told him there was no fix for this, with funding being his primary issue. His lighthouse wasn't fully developed when he took action and left his job. He was looking only at the passion portion of his lighthouse and failed to build the proper outlook for his future based upon all the required elements before he took action. He had courage, and he identified a passion, but he did not take a look at his family and their economic situation, their financial lighthouse, to determine whether they were ready to take the salary cut needed for him to follow his passion. He didn't do the required research on the industry he was moving into to determine whether it could create the income he needed to support his family's financial demands. I expressed to him that his passion doesn't have to be fulfilled by his career, but his career and high earnings can fund his ability to exercise his passion.

His career must be the greatest utilization of skill sets and abilities and have the ability to support his family based upon their current needs. Either that or they need to be ready to experience extreme sacrifice and drastically lower their lifestyle. He admitted that his previous role was where he felt his skill sets were leveraged for greatness, but he was restless and wanted to chase a dream of his passions. After multiple meetings with me, he returned to his prior career and sold or shut down the gyms for a loss. This is one of many stories I can share that support the fact that passion and courage are not enough and that these often fail and leave entrepreneurs frustrated, burned out, and in dire financial straits.

Having a limited scope or lens on your lighthouse can lead to countless issues and failures in your life. Finding and developing your lighthouse goes way beyond passion and courage. I want you to be in touch with your passions, and courage will be required to take action, but these two alone are not enough to find the success you're capable of. This book is structured to help you build your foundation, remove the elements that hold you back, and find success based on who you are. In his book *So Good They Can't Ignore You*, Georgetown professor and author Cal Newport discusses the requirements for jobs and careers and the fact that you must have the opportunity to distinguish yourself through your skills and abilities but also be able to develop those skills further and thrive while doing so. If your passions drive you toward a business, industry, career, or job that allows you to thrive due to your skills and abilities, then it's a great pairing and may be a fantastic answer for you. However, the process still requires you to take into consideration the entire development of your lighthouse and your goals.

It is not just about a job, career, industry, or business; you have to make sure to connect with why you are driven, who you are, and what you want to achieve or become. When I was a cop, I was trying to figure out how to get to a better version of myself and set goals for a brighter future. I worked hard to determine my best skill sets and abilities and then identified what industry would allow me to reach my lighthouse. My passions were not for the industry I found myself in or that I focused on but were grounded in the core elements I had identified. I was focused on working with people, impacting lives, providing opportunities for employees and team members, and building a scalable business that could provide specific financial results throughout my life.

The industry I landed in that matched the goals I was chasing was the financial industry. It seemed like something that would make me want to hit my head against the wall just thinking about it, but it lined up with all the requirements for who I was and where I wanted to go. As I moved further into this industry, I became passionate about it. I was able to break down all the walls and connect all the ways my passions could be fulfilled through it. Being able to use my greatest skill sets and leverage this industry to increase my ability to impact people's lives while having super financial results was the equation for my success. It also allowed me to connect with entrepreneurs, help change their forever, change the course of many financially unstable families to become financially independent, and constantly work to grow a bigger reach. I connected my best skill sets and reverse-engineered my way into my passions through an industry that provided all the requirements for my lighthouse.

Now, as an entrepreneur for over sixteen years, at the time of writing this book, I have found great success, fulfillment, and growth throughout these years. I will be honest with you—the vision for my lighthouse has constantly adapted, and the development of who I am has been substantial. Financial freedom only gives me more hunger and drive to continue the scope of my impact and development of my skills. I have multiple successful businesses that are all a part of my journey toward my lighthouse, and everything I put my time, effort, and energy into is for the lighthouse I am chasing.

My fully discovered passion is to impact your life and the lives of every reader, entrepreneur, executive and client I can reach. I have now connected with the fact that just finding a level of success through the financial industry is not enough anymore, and I am hungry for a bigger reach and a larger impact. The opportunity to write this book and chase after other opportunities that are now in my lighthouse would never have been in front of me if I hadn't walked down these specific roads and achieved success throughout my life.

So, through working the exact process I am walking you through in this book, I've been able to leverage my passions within business and hit greater achievements than my original lighthouse, all while developing a greater version of my goals and a definition of my success. I have found that my deep-rooted passions were not the surface-level ones I initially connected with.

These original passions are stepping stones that get you to connect with what you are really excited about. *The perfect pairing is when passions, courage, and abilities all line-up and become an unstoppable force in your life.* In my life and the lives of many others I have worked with, I have found that when you drive hard toward a lighthouse based on who you are and what you are built to be, the passions connect on the journey.

Clarifying the Core Elements of Your Lighthouse

Your lighthouse must be built on the core of who you are, as well as the important elements of future successes and outcomes in your life. I want to walk you through some critical questions that you should work through and dig deep into as you define your lighthouse. I have also put together additional resources to assist you that are available on the resource page, which the link is at the end of this book.

The **first core element** is the focus you will incorporate for your future success. Many people have different definitions of success, and defining what it is to you and your life is pertinent to clarifying your lighthouse. For some, there is a major focus on financial freedom or financial success. Freedom of time is a pressing element to others, and they are driven to remove the pressure of time requirements and obligations that fill their calendars. Many people are driven based on relationships and the ability to build and develop them freely. Others focus heavily on developing purpose, so their lighthouse is based on finding fulfillment. Some are driven by the freedom to chase their passions.

Freedom of location is a massive lighthouse to many who feel as though they are tied to specific cities or areas due to obligations with work, family, or other commitments. These examples represent various elements that are incorporated into many people's lighthouses. It's important to note that these focuses are not about picking one over the other. Instead, your lighthouse and the goals you set should fit the future you aspire to build and can include as many elements as you feel driven to pursue.

What is the greatest version of you that you are chasing? This is a haunting question and a major reason for always adjusting and updating my lighthouse. This is the **second core element** for you to work through as you lay out plans and set your lighthouse:

- What does this look like to you?
- How does this version of you show up?

- What can this person achieve?
- What has or will this person accomplish and overcome?
- What will this person go after and take on in their life?
- What do you want to be known for?

These are all hard questions and will require you to take the time to work through each one to set well-rounded goals within your lighthouse. This can never be focused on one specific element—you have to look at your lighthouse from a multi-angled perspective.

The balance required here is making sure you are pushing hard toward what you define as success while constantly developing in the direction of the greatest version of you that you are dedicated to becoming. As you set your lighthouse and lay out the goals for your future, you have to work through these questions to find your focus. In the end, it is vital to be proud of what you've accomplished and confident in who you've become.

The **third core element** of massive importance for your lighthouse is how you will show up for those who are a part of your driving forces. When you read through Chapter 4, you learned that there are aspects of the people in your life that are a part of your *why* and your driving forces:

- In what ways are you going to show up and become the best version of yourself for those people?
- How do you want to impact the people closest to you?
- Who needs you to show up as the best version of yourself, and what does that look like?

In my life, I'm dedicated to showing up in a way that's an example for my kids. I want to show them that no matter what life throws at you, there's nothing you can't handle. Your future is not defined by the difficulties you face. You have the ability to always go hard after your life with your long-term goals in front of you.

The greatest version of who I am and what I'm going to show my children is that I'm relentless, I'm not afraid to step outside of my comfort zone, I'm willing to take risks to achieve greatness, and I'm dedicated to impacting people by being the greatest example of constant improvement and achievement. I want to show them that despite all the odds against them, they can break through their cracked lenses and push themselves to greatness. I want to be an example of going after life with greater relentlessness than the hardships life sends at me.

In your life, if you've identified specific individuals as part of your driving forces, those for whom you want to show up and who inspire you, you must also define the goals and lighthouses you're setting for yourself. Determining what these aspirations look like for you and those around you is crucial.

These elements all have their purpose and importance in the development of the lighthouse you will chase after and set as your guide for your long-term success. Each one is a part of your lighthouse and should be configured into it, but make sure you are laying the foundation with a widespread outlook across all of these rather than a fixation on just one.

There is a consistent theme of some people focusing on their lighthouses but mainly on financial elements. Be sure to work through all the elements above, and don't just get stuck focused on the shiny financial objects. Your lighthouse requires that you push yourself to develop in the direction of your greatness. You must have a lighthouse that will bring you fulfillment when you reach your end goals as well as throughout the process.

This is all about thriving through the journey and enjoying the growth and development. Knowing that you're moving forward and having a reach that is greater than you is key to your success. Chasing money alone will leave you empty and hold you back from achieving your greatest potential.

I've seen countless wealthy individuals who are bitter, angry, and resentful. They had money and finance as their core lighthouse. They missed the mark on the different aspects of what achievement and greatness look like, and even though they experienced everything money had to offer, they were left empty and dissatisfied. Your goals and your lighthouse must go beyond just your financial aspirations. They have to align with who you are built to be. Push yourself beyond what you feel you might be able to achieve as the current version of you.

As you work toward setting your lighthouse, it is essential to work through this chapter and connect back to other elements we have covered. Make sure you are not limiting the goals and future you are capable of achieving. See yourself for who you really are and connect with your greatest abilities, skill sets, and driving forces as catalysts in your life.

If you don't take the time to set your lighthouse and focus on who you want to be and what you want to accomplish, the lack of results will leave you unsatisfied. You have to be willing to come up with goals beyond anything you feel comfortable with and start driving forward to a future that might seem impossible right now. The setting of your lighthouse and the excitement of seeing your future for what it could become should be thrilling, even with all the unknowns and knowing what the process will require of you.

This is all a part of your journey, all part of the story of your life. Your future cannot be built off you being settled and taking the easy roads. If you settle and set your lighthouse based upon your fears and other holdbacks, it will leave you with regrets, failure, and a story that you are ashamed for others to read. Take the time to develop your lighthouse and your goals. *This is your one life to live, and there are no redos, so make this one count.*

This chapter covers a lot of information and contains many things you must work through. The resources page is an excellent place to find additional support, worksheets, and videos. I am dedicated to impacting your life, and that is why I want to go beyond the normal scope of just writing a book.

www.SuckLessDoBetterBook.com/Resources

CHAPTER 7

The Truth of Your Reality

A look of concern flooded his face as I explained to him that, as a client and friend, I cared too much about his future to lend him the large sum of money he was asking for. I voiced my firm belief in not mixing business and personal relationships by giving out loans and also expressed my concern about many of the decisions I had seen him make. I explained that giving him a six-figure loan would not only create more issues but would not fix the core problems that had gotten him to this point. He stormed out of my office as though I was the cause of his financial troubles and had created the situation he was facing.

The truth is that he had reached a small level of success through his hustle, drive, and hunger, which was enough to send his ego into a tailspin of expensive cars, flashy jewelry, fine clothes, and a highly pampered wife. His focus had been on looking like a multi-millionaire rather than becoming one. It was extremely evident that his flashy lifestyle was at risk, and his wife's comfort was being challenged.

Earlier in our conversation, I had walked him through the prior strategies, warnings, and other previous discussions where I had warned him that he would find himself in this situation if he didn't make changes. I expressed to him the importance of working on the plan I had helped him create to get himself out of this current situation. Over the next year, I watched as he desperately entered business partnerships and ravaged them financially like a swarm of locusts out of control in a field of crops. He leveraged his persona of being highly successful to pry his way into opportunities, and he used his swagger to convince business owners that he was their gateway to future success. With his overpromising and underdelivering on every engagement, as well as the constant need to identify new "prey," those closest to him became extremely concerned. This behavior and his actions caused him to lose his closest friendships, business relationships, and those who had supported him in his launch to the initial success he had experienced.

His actions had caused others financial hardship, damaged businesses, and left him with a wake of severed relationships along with a bad reputation and a long list of failures. It would be clear to anyone that it was time for a change and a reality check. His attention should have been hyperfocused on taking advice, warnings, and guidance to heart, but instead, he was living in a false reality that kept him in his destructive cycle.

I would love to give you an update that he has since changed and is now in recovery mode, but the last I heard is that his path has had nothing but similar results as his desperation increases and his reach shrinks. He is trying to pull talent from businesses where he was once a partner and is constantly scrambling to pull together the money to maintain a lifestyle he fell into. His desperation to keep up the appearance of his success early on in his entrepreneurial journey leaves him making desperate decisions that leave a trail of hardships behind him that others must deal with.

You need to understand this because each one of us is vulnerable to falling into our own cycle. The moment that you are unwilling to see the truth of your reality is the start of the road toward your ultimate failure and demise. You have to always maintain a connection with the reality of where you are, the results of your actions, and the truth of your past. Your ability to connect to both your past and current performance will affect your ability to reach your lighthouse.

You are moving toward an understanding of the process to achieve your greatest potential, and it requires you to take the time to inventory your results, efforts, and actions and determine how they line up with your lighthouse. These all have to be viewed in a different light now that you have fully connected to your driving forces, worked through your broken lenses, and identified the clarity of your strengths and vision for your future. The reality check you must make is to look at your current and past actions through the vantage point of your lighthouse and take inventory of which will gain momentum toward your now clarified goals.

Be Honest With Yourself

Your future success will be determined by your ability to be honest with yourself and take ownership of your current reality and each subsequent move throughout your life. The *future you* relies on the *present you* to be honest about your current efforts as well as the actions you're taking on a daily basis. You have to analyze the results that your life is producing and determine whether they are enough to get you to your lighthouse.

As you look at your life, it's vital to look at the efforts you're concentrating on. Are they focused and dedicated to your lighthouse? Are they pushing you to gain momentum toward your end goals? Are they producing results in line with the movement toward the greatest version of you? Your life's focused attention and current efforts must always align with your long-term focus and goals. The lighthouse that you set is your guide and desired outcome. Are you taking the necessary actions and keeping your focus?

Like many people, you might pride yourself in being a hustler, someone always willing to put in the hard work and do whatever it takes to succeed. The truth is that this doesn't equate to true success and often won't get you to your lighthouse because of distractions and shiny objects that derail the momentum. You have to channel that hustle and focus your efforts toward the future goals you have in place. Dedicate yourself to developing the greatest version of yourself. Most people who consider themselves hustlers are driven, ambitious, and dedicated but have a convoluted or missing focus. Have you been living with the pinball style of output rather than the dragster approach? This will lead to a lot of movement, but it won't necessarily get you to the end result you want. Every entrepreneur I encounter is at a different place or level in their journey. When they're honest with themselves, there's always an inventory of wasted focus and wasted efforts. Look inward and connect with these hustler-type mentalities and determine how focused your efforts have been throughout your experience as an entrepreneur.

There have been many times when I've put energy and effort in the wrong direction. I had to adjust my focus and realize it was nothing but a distraction derailing me from progressing toward my lighthouse. I call these distractions in entrepreneurs' lives "shiny objects," and the majority of entrepreneurs I come across all suffer from "shiny object syndrome." The syndrome is a combination of the excitement running through our system for the pursuit of business and dedication to our goals mixed with our constant desire for future-focused action. In your life, what shiny objects are keeping you distracted rather than focused on the actions and the vehicle that will get you to your destination? A major part of why we set a lighthouse and chase a long-term goal is to make sure we have a bar against which we can measure every opportunity or shiny object. Having a precisely defined track to run on with a designated and defined destination gives you a clear vision of the direction in which you are moving. This allows you to identify the tracks that align and those that derail.

Most entrepreneurs run at life with a very unstructured lighthouse approach focused only on money. They're trying to find success without clear goals or even a definition of what success looks like. They jump from opportunity to opportunity, trying to find the one that will make them more money and chasing a golden rainbow and unicorns that don't exist. In the midst of their rat race chasing these shiny objects and pipe dreams, they find burnout, major distractions, destruction of relationships, and a lot of wasted time. Author and motivational speaker Jim Rohn said it well: "Motivation alone is not enough. If you have an idiot and you motivate him, now you have a motivated idiot." You need to ground yourself in your reality and reflect on your past. Take inventory of the shiny objects that have distracted you on your entrepreneurial journey. Identify and list the times when you lacked focus on your now clearly defined goals.

Take a look at your past roadmap:
- What does it look like?
- Where have you been, and what areas do you have to change to create a better future for yourself?
- What part of your past has achieved the best results?
- Where have you found great outcomes that can be a part of your future momentum toward your long-term goals?
- What part of the drive and ambition has aligned with your now-defined lighthouse?
- What lessons can you look back on and learn from to build a better toolbox of knowledge for this next leg of your journey chasing your future?

I really connect with a quote from John C. Maxwell: "A man must be big enough to admit his mistakes, smart enough to profit from them, and strong enough to correct them." Looking back and working through these questions should be a part of the development of who you can become and what your future can look like as long as you're honest about your past.

For some of you, the honest look back on your life might be full of the choices you made to chase the easy roads you traveled by showing up as a lesser version of yourself. What are the decisions you've made that have stunted your growth because the road might have looked a little bit more difficult, a little bit more challenging? Those easy roads don't push you. They don't require you to develop yourself to your full potential. Hard work pays off, and this is true in every area of your life. Hard work in relationships and putting effort into people you care about creates better relationships. If you're trying to get ripped and build strength, it requires hard work and dedication at the gym. If you want to run marathons, you have to put in the hard work and pound the pavement for hours to train to even enter a race. So why would your career, entrepreneurship, and the financial side of your life not require dedication and development of greatness? Hard work will never be in vain when it's focused on the right cause, which is your lighthouse.

I've experienced firsthand entrepreneurs like yourself who deal with a serious burnout phase filled with frustration and a lack of progress. Many times, it's caused by some of these things we just discussed—shiny objects, past decisions to stay on the easy road, and continuous movement in the wrong direction. You, as an entrepreneur, need to be open to the reality that you might be burned out by your bad decisions, the effort you've put in to just keep your head above water, or chasing the wrong roads. Your situation is no different from using the wrong tool for the wrong purpose in construction. You might have a power tool, but when used for the wrong purpose, it can be destructive and harmful, and you might destroy the tool or whatever you're working on. You must know who you are and what you're built for and make sure you're putting the right effort in the right direction with the right purpose to achieve the right end result.

The great part of the journey that I've been on is that I have endless stories of entrepreneurial success and failures that I can pull from my mental database to share with you throughout this process. There are so many entrepreneurs who have chased the hard roads—but in the entirely wrong direction. Some were focused on the wrong industry or those without scalability. Others lacked focus and were constantly running in completely different directions all over the place with shiny object syndrome. Too many entrepreneurs are sitting in the grind but never take the time or have the opportunity to understand the principles I have laid out in this book, and they are constantly finding themselves in their suck.

There is a blessing and an obligation that comes from my seat as an adviser to many entrepreneurs. The hard conversations are challenging and full of tough love. I am built with a passion to build people up and help them find their full potential. This requires me to be a firm voice that speaks truth to those who are not giving their life their best effort and are instead chasing their tails or choosing to take the easy roads.

There's a client in one of our financial businesses that I was rather impressed with when I first met him eight or ten years ago. He had natural communication skills, swag, and a quick, off-the-line success in launching his business. I was sure that this guy was destined for greatness. To be honest with you, I was a bit jealous of his confidence and the way he carried himself. He seemed to understand the equation for greatness and have his future at his fingertips. I had a conversation with him about two months ago, and he had not gone any further with his business or success since we first met. His business hadn't scaled, and his life hadn't moved any further down the path toward greatness. He had been distracted by shiny objects and had a complete lack of a lighthouse. He also didn't have anybody in his life who would call him on the carpet about his raw abilities and skills and how he was completely wasting his potential.

As I sat down with him, I expressed honestly that I was shocked that after this long in business, he hadn't completely conquered the market, achieved ridiculous success, or gone on to do something great. I explained to him that with his raw potential, killer swag, excellent communication skills, and natural abilities, he should have been running circles around every entrepreneur I had met. He had all this potential but had wasted the last ten years. He said he'd had some small roadblocks and difficulties, and I told him that's where grit and relentlessness should kick in, that you can't let anything get in your way. Through our conversation, I helped him understand that he began in an industry that wasn't suited to his natural strengths and aspirations, and as a result, he found it challenging to fully exercise his goals and ambitions.

Another big issue we discussed is that from the start of his business, he chased the easy answer and a quick fix financially. He launched his business, which got him to a point where he could pay his bills and have a little comfort, but it didn't provide any long-term growth. It didn't get him to his lighthouse. As I'm sure you can understand, the conversation was a little awkward, completely caught him off guard, and gave him a glimpse of how he was viewed by the outside entrepreneurial community. I will tell you that he took this conversation on the chin and connected with the fact that he has more potential than what he was exercising. I hope to fill you in later on the super success that he decided to chase after, but right now, he is still in the process. He's working through the exact principles I am providing for you in this book to help him identify what he is built for so that he can set goals and create his own lighthouse.

The same is true for you. You need to take inventory of who you are, what you're built for, and what you're chasing. You have to look at your life and connect with your failures and shortcomings and the fact that you are built to reach greatness. Stop running in the wrong direction and take the time to be honest with yourself about where you are in life and whether your current path will lead you to your lighthouse. You can want a better future for yourself, but without the right actions, there is only failure in your path.

The Future on Your Current Path

What will your future look like if you maintain your current path, level of effort, dedication, drive, ambition, focus, and decision-making? Look at your future for a moment through the lens of your past results and actions. What will the outcome be if you don't go after your future with a different perspective, approach, and methodology? Will the results from your past get you to the lighthouse you're chasing? Are these results the greatest version of you? Is this going to get you the success that you're hungry for? Look at your past and ask yourself if that same effort and action will achieve the desired results. You are not alone—even the greatest entrepreneurs look at their past and understand it was a learning experience and there is a better future version of the person who has shown up in the past.

What areas do you need to focus on to make sure that the results you end up with give you a better future than where you currently are? Your future, your lighthouse, and the greatest version of you require you to do something different. This book is the roadmap to break you out of your past and pave the way to your best future. You have to look at the reality of who you have been and how you have shown up in the past. Through that lens, compare it to who you are built to be and what you are capable of becoming and decide which version of you will be carried into your future.

Is It the Driver or the Vehicle?

Reviewing your past and doing a reality check is not just about who you have been and how you have shown up but also about looking at the vehicle you chose to chase your success. Your vehicle is your job, business, career, or industry that you're chasing as an entrepreneur or motivated individual. There is a required pairing based on the driver's skill sets and abilities and the capabilities of the vehicle. You have to work through all the processes laid out in Chapter 5 to fully connect with who you are and what you are built for, as well as have your lighthouse fully identified to determine whether there is the right connection between you and your vehicle. Reflecting back on your greatest abilities, your skill sets, your best utilization of these, and your 20 percent is the vehicle you're driving based upon your ability to maximize all of these? Connect back to why you are in this job, business, career, or industry. Does it connect to the person you are built to be?

The lighthouse you're chasing, and the goals you have now set should be your guide to determining the right vehicle. Does the vehicle you are currently in, or the one you are considering chasing, have the ability to get you to the outcome, success, financial freedom, and greatness that you are capable of?

Are you trying to drive a monster truck on a NASCAR track—lots of power but the wrong vehicle for the race? So many entrepreneurs I work with have great skills and abilities but use the wrong vehicle to achieve their goals. Many times, they're taking action on industries that are easier to get into or businesses that are faster to launch rather than working through the process of determining the right vehicle based on who they are and the goals they have laid out for themselves. Other entrepreneurs chase and follow somebody else's path, dream, or vision rather than developing their own.

In both situations, these entrepreneurs have to face reality at some point. After multiple failures, they come to the realization that they are not chasing their own lighthouse and they are not using the right vehicle. This leaves them feeling empty, failing, and stuck on a path they were never built to be on. You might be in a current struggle dealing with debt, responsibilities, and the pressures that come from life and the vehicle you're driving. Your track and the race you're running might be one that's pushing you toward your suck rather than moving you toward your lighthouse. Take the time to reflect and determine whether it's an issue with the driver or the vehicle.

I've seen many entrepreneurs almost give up completely on their journey because of this very issue. They've been driving the wrong vehicle throughout their entire career. Too many driven and motivated individuals are living in the wrong career or running the wrong business because they have settled into comfort rather than chasing the greatest version of themselves and focusing on their lighthouse. Most have never connected with the principles in this book and don't understand that a relationship must be made between the vehicle and the driver. What does this look like in your life? Maybe you've accepted security over taking the difficult roads to achieve the success that you are capable of. Are you struggling because you have become comfortable with complacency? You have to understand that each decision you make that moves you toward comfort, security, and an easy road is one more movement that kills your inner entrepreneurial spirit, drive, and ambition. This time of reflection is needed for you to look back at your life and see where your decisions derailed you.

For those of you who are feeling unsettled, have realized that what you are driving will never get you to your lighthouse, and are ready to take action toward moving to a different vehicle, it's important first to identify all your issues as the driver. Make sure you don't bring all your problems into your next vehicle. If you're never honest with yourself about your issues, it won't matter what vehicle you're driving. You have to be completely honest and accept your failures, weaknesses, and areas of needed improvement in your life. You need to know the strengths, abilities, and skill sets that are a part of your catalyst to achieve your greatest success. You must be willing to put in the work. This means implementing every principle in this book and utilizing all of the resources provided. Set your lighthouse, connect with who you really are, gather your fuel, and choose the vehicle that will get you to the success you desire.

Planner, Person of Action, or Both?

Reflecting on your past and accepting the truth of your reality can be difficult for many, but it's vital to leverage this truth for growth and development. Ensuring you are directing your efforts in the right direction and using the right vehicle is crucial. This reflection includes identifying whether you are a planner, a person of action, or both. Connecting to the reality of where you sit will help you determine where some of the holdbacks in your journey may be. *Your life is a constant adaptation based upon new information and knowledge that you have to absorb and take in.* Planning is necessary to connect new information and the actions you need to take. There is a crippling effect that occurs in many people after the information is absorbed and the actions identified. They fail to implement and take the action steps needed to turn the planning into reality. In some cases, people take quick action in areas of comfort or interest but hesitate or fail to act when faced with challenges or something in which they lack interest. There's a tendency for fast action in areas of greatest interest, while follow-up and development may be lacking in areas of hardship or difficulty.

As an entrepreneur and a driven, motivated individual, you don't have the ability to pick and choose the required actions you're going to take. You don't have the option of not chasing and taking action in difficult areas. If that's how you operate, you'll be left with major weaknesses and inevitably run in circles. This will leave you void of the success and greatness you are dialing in for your life through your planning. You have to be real about your willingness to not just talk about and plan but to take action.

You may be a person of action but miss a portion of the planning and find yourself without the tools or foundation necessary to succeed. Are you taking premature action and not taking the time to get the right planning in place to make sure you will succeed through the process? Take a deep look at where your process gets jammed, held up, or derailed. No one is exempt from this. We're all struggling to find a balance, as each of us has a natural strength that's greater in one of these two areas. Make it a point to be real with yourself about where you are struggling, whether you need to take action despite holdups and difficulties or take additional steps in the planning process to make sure you don't act too fast.

The combination of these is vital for your future. It's important to take the time to plan and create your action steps, as well as be dedicated to executing the needed steps without delay or hesitation. So, as you take inventory of your reality, accept the truth of where you currently are with this balance. Planner, person of action, or both—there isn't a right or a wrong but rather just an understanding of who you are so you can grow and challenge yourself in the area that doesn't come naturally. Your success requires you to be both a planner and a person of action. Connecting to the truth of your current reality is pivotal as you continue to chase after your lighthouse.

Built to Be Versus What You Have Allowed

The reality you find yourself in is not necessarily a reflection of who you were built to be but rather of who you have allowed yourself to become. It's crucial to recognize the difference between these two states, as allowing the past to define the present can be a major concern. We all have the ability to choose our future and develop ourselves into a greater version of what has shown up in our pasts. No matter what you have failed at, what truly matters is your lighthouse and the future goals you feel driven toward. Yes, you must make sure you see your current situation for what it is and accept your mistakes and weaknesses. Failures are learning experiences, and distractions from the past are now visible so that you don't get derailed again. The issues you faced have been developed into knowledge to conquer future roadblocks. Your weaknesses are now surface-level for you to accept and counter.

Connect with who you are, the history of where you've been, and the reality of your flaws, and focus on building off that foundation. *You cannot keep going after life the same way that you have been and expect to get greater results.* You have to determine the actions that will increase momentum toward your now fully identified lighthouse versus the actions that will distract you or keep you in your suck. Be completely real with yourself and brutally honest, even to the point where reality might hurt your pride. A vital part of this process is knowing the core of your strengths and where you can create change for your future and acknowledging the weaknesses and actions holding you back on a daily basis. You have to dig deep and define the 20 percent where you thrive and get the greatest results rather than being stuck in the suck of the 80 percent that's holding you back. Only when you are completely honest with yourself will you gain the peace that comes with acknowledging these truths.

You cannot fall back into your suck. You must move forward toward the person that you were built to be; you must suck less and do better every day. Being honest with yourself about your holdbacks and demons from the past is crucial, as they may be preventing you from becoming the person you aspire to be. Push hard to break free from your past, the issues in your lenses, and the distractions that derail your progress. Conquer the past and learn from your mistakes rather than wallowing in them. The wrong directions you took because of the shiny object you chased. The trauma that causes you to define yourself as less than the greatness you are. The excuses you hide behind prevent you from rising to your full potential. The enemies that you let torment you. The inner voice that's pulling you back to your failures rather than letting you focus on your successes. That's the draw to your suck rather than a focus on your lighthouse. Expect greater results from yourself. Work through the darkness that torments you and the hardships that hold you back, and break free to align with the future you're chasing.

So I ask, who you are meant to be versus who you've allowed yourself to become? You are built for more. You have underutilized your capabilities and accepted less of yourself throughout your journey thus far. The person you are built to be has the ability to channel your past and where you are in your life and develop you to greatness. Stop accepting less from yourself and push hard into the full capabilities within you.

Do You Have What It Takes?

With no fairy godmother to "abracadabra" all your wants and dreams, and no magical formulas to follow to gain success, you have to rely on a system to guide you. Part of that discovery needs to be identifying core traits or principles that are vital to leverage to chase down and achieve the success you are built for. You can often identify consistent attributes and themes in those who have succeeded and found greatness through their journey. These individuals are driven, ambitious, dedicated, relentless through hardships, resilient despite obstacles, honest about their strengths and weaknesses, and aware of their mistakes and failures. They connect and leverage their strengths, skill sets, and abilities. They have grit and are dedicated to constantly improving who they are. These are just some of the qualities and attributes you will find in those who have found true success, including the individuals I listed in Chapter 3 and so many more I have encountered.

Through the process of connecting with the reality of where you currently are, how are you showing up with these qualities and principles? Where do you sit in the willingness to grow and develop yourself? You have to determine whether you have what it takes to hit your success and chase after your future with the tenacity required to reach your lighthouse.

If you follow the roadmap of this book, the trajectory of your future can vastly change. You have to take the time to put the right action steps in place and work through each and every process listed throughout this book. You know that there are no shortcuts to your success, but a roadmap makes clear the direct path and fast-tracks you to get the results and desired outcomes. Be driven and motivated to take daily actions toward who you are dedicated to becoming and the lighthouse you set out to achieve. Your next steps on the road to success start with fully connecting to your current reality and identifying the exact areas in which you need to develop and grow. The ability to suck less and do better each day requires you to be connected to your present situation and the hard truths of a tough reality.

CHAPTER 8

Identify Your Competition

As I met with eight other entrepreneurs to discuss our businesses and the momentum we had gained, my frustrations continued to build. When these guys talked about their fast growth and goals for the future months, I felt like I was getting kicked in the stomach. I thought my growth was great, but it wasn't keeping up with some of these guys' businesses. The plans I had put together weren't getting the same results. I knew there would be a difference because we were all in unrelated industries, but I wasn't prepared for this moment of mental defeat. This group of entrepreneurs had been meeting since shortly after we all started our businesses, and we got together to discuss the hardships and roadblocks we were facing and support each other. Some of these individuals had turned it into a competitive situation, focusing on who was experiencing the fastest growth and whose revenues and earnings were reaching specific milestones. Each meeting became more of a flex for some of these guys, a place to boost their self-worth.

During my first three years in business, these meetings greatly impacted how I felt about myself as an entrepreneur and my ability to succeed. There were times when I even second-guessed my plan and business model and considered making an adjustment. There was a specific moment after one meeting when I had to take a huge step back, sit down and go back to my initial business model to determine whether it was still the best route to get to my lighthouse. I broke down all the reasons I chose the industry I did, the way I structured my business, the engagement styles I decided to use with my clients, and my long-term plans for my business. I connected back to the fact that the industry in which I was building a business was stable and consistent with minimal fluctuation, and I had built a model for consistent growth.

My model was a foundation-building business that would continue to build and grow and have the ability to become unstoppable. I was not building a sexy, get-rich-quick type of business but rather a business that not only could be consistent with high profits but was also a sellable business that was becoming an asset with a high valuation. The business process and the plan I had built could not compete with other industries' faster off-the-line model, but it was focused on the long term and growth over time. I had to connect back to all the reasons and the lighthouse I had set out to accomplish with the business I had created.

Through this process, I had to connect with the fact that I cannot compete with anyone else. I had to shut out the noise around me and focus on chasing my lighthouse. It became clear that comparing others' journeys to mine is impossible. They have different purposes, visions, desired outcomes, planning, and long-term outputs. It was evident that it was not even possible to compete with any of these guys—we were all running different races.

The next meeting came, and as the competitive comments started to come out, I found myself not even connecting with them. I communicated that the group was not designed to be a competition but rather a support group, and I expressed the frustrations I had to work through. This conversation led to others being open about their struggle with the competition mentality, and we were able to remove this from the group going forward and focus on the support aspect that was the group's original intent.

During the last sixteen years, I have seen some of those guys have major financial hardships, lose businesses, and have to start over because of their type of business, their business model, the economy, and even decisions that stemmed from their arrogance. Some have not been able to release the competition mindset and have separated themselves from the group.

The competition mentality can become a destructive slippery slope that will eat you alive and create an unhealthy pattern in your life. There is enough success to go around. We can use the momentum in our own lives to help encourage and support those around us who are on their own journey toward their own success.

I had to stop comparing my situation and my business to others. The roads we were traveling and the goals we were chasing were completely different. Cutting out that distraction, focusing on my lighthouse and goals, and defining the success I was and still am chasing was freeing. It's a mindset that you must keep pushing yourself to stay focused on. The results I have achieved within my years as an entrepreneur have been way beyond anything the earlier version of myself could have imagined. It was only achievable by having focused efforts, dedication, goals, and a direction based on my driving forces and desired outcome. If I had continued to live in competition or comparison to others, I would have derailed and missed the lighthouse I was chasing. I would have found myself back in my suck.

The same is true for you. The competition in your life must be between the *prior version* of you and the *current version* of you. You have to focus on your lighthouse, your goals, and the greatest version of you that you're driving toward. Push yourself daily to achieve results that will gain momentum in that direction. You should have requirements, expectations, goals, and a bar to reach. Focus on the movements needed to achieve those results. The comparison and competition should only be about you and how you're showing up each day to move the needle forward in your life toward your lighthouse and how you need to show up to achieve your planned goals and future.

Remove the Noise

When chasing the life you want, you have to identify potential areas of distraction and outside influence that can change the focus of your competition with yourself. These areas are the noise around you that needs to be silenced or removed from your life. You must be fully aware of potential distractions and understand how to use discernment throughout your journey. Removing the noise will keep you focused on your life, goals, and lighthouse. If not silenced, it can derail your progress and your desired outcome.

Social media, as an example, is a major source of noise that can derail you from focusing on your lighthouse. You might constantly compare yourself to the people you see on social media. This may be based on their claims of success, results, physical appearance, or business ventures. When this comparison happens, try to connect to the fact that the goals you set for yourself are based on who you are and what you want to achieve. People on social media put out there only what they want others to see.

Most of the time, a false reality is presented. In working with many entrepreneurs and executives, some of whom post on social media, I have seen the fake realities presented. In many cases, what's posted are direct lies. I have seen CEOs post claims of great business growth and scaling of their companies while their businesses are on a downward trend and going through major financial difficulties. I've actually fired coaching clients for the lies about their successes that they've put out on social media. The only true way for them to succeed is to stop living in a false reality and quit claiming they've already achieved their goals.

You are not in competition with anyone on social media. You must face the reality that your success requires you to focus on yourself. You compete only with yourself, and don't have room for negativity to slip into your mind when comparing yourself to others, especially when you know the false picture that so many people are painting on social media.

There are other places where noise can come from. Sometimes, these places can be disguised as very positive momentum-building arenas, but if they don't align with your lighthouse and who you are, then they can become your distraction. Some examples are Facebook groups, mastermind groups, or business development groups based on topics or business ideas that are not in line with your long-term goals. To be more specific, maybe your lighthouse is based upon maximizing your abilities in real estate and becoming a real estate investor, but at one point, you thought about starting a dropshipping company and joined groups that would help you down this path. If you determine this is no longer part of your lighthouse, then cut it out. It's nothing but noise and a distraction.

I constantly tell myself and my clients if something is not fueling you toward competing with yourself but is creating distractions and comparisons to others, then you need to cut it out. This might mean disconnecting from social media or removing yourself from situations or groups that have the potential to distract or derail you from your future success. You have to take the time to identify each area of your life that might be the noise that's distracting you and make a move to eliminate it.

The main idea behind this is that you must be confident in who you are and know the lighthouse you are headed toward. In your journey through this book thus far, you have connected with the foundation of how you are built and the goals you are striving to achieve. The distractions in your life need to be silenced, and the greatest version of you has to show up to hit the goals you have set for yourself.

Cut out the Expectations and the Comparisons From Others.

The crushing weight of expectations that others put on you and the comparisons that become the judgment of who you are in other people's eyes derails you on your journey to the person you are striving to be. To acknowledge these in your life is a major part of your growth, and to ensure that these don't create distractions, you must identify the relationships that are the source and create the boundaries that will remove the constant push or pull. *Your life should be developed based on the principles of who you are and what you are built for, not the expectations from others or comparisons to others.* You have to live up to the standards you put in place for yourself based upon the greatest version of you that can show up. The expectations and comparisons from other people will create issues and distractions and hinder you from achieving your lighthouse as long as you allow them to continue.

This will require you to review the relationships in your life and set boundaries with those who have created unnecessary competition or put their own expectations on you. You also have to work through the relationships from your past that have created these expectations that are engraved into your mind. Some of these are a part of the broken lenses in your life that you have to work through and constantly keep in check. In this process, you have to make sure that you're staying focused on the road in front of you and dedicated to competing with the you that showed up yesterday. You are called to always work to better yourself and move your progress down the pathway toward the lighthouse that you know you can achieve.

Another issue that needs to be addressed is that there's often a deep-rooted wiring in you that needs to be corrected. You were trained as a child to listen to others and the requirements, rules, and expectations placed upon you. As you continued through your childhood, there were moments where the expectations led to comparisons in our families, friend groups, and even church groups. Parenting and discipline are a natural part of life, and the fact that your parents set standards, boundaries, and requirements and you were required to follow the rules is quite normal. However, there are times when families take this to another level and create additional issues by allowing competition or comparisons to be present.

Parents can be a catalyst that creates this comparison and competition mentality. From early on, some of you might have heard comments like, "Why can't you be like your brother or sister? They finished all their chores, they ate all their food, they didn't argue, they got their homework done." Parents don't realize that they start the spiral of comparison with comments like these. It creates a major issue of expectations tied to other people rather than each one of us identifying our own skill sets and abilities and setting the bar for what we are capable of, not others. In households with multiple kids, there are already dynamics between siblings that create competition and expectations from each other. Parents often fuel this fire with their comments, which can exacerbate issues between siblings.

In your childhood, these expectations, comparisons, and competitions are extended and layered throughout your education. It doesn't matter whether you're in private or public school growing up; the level and type of expectation placed on each child becomes the bar that is set and normalized, and it is not based on you or your learning abilities. You are required to adapt to a preconceived notion of who you are, and to be accepted; you must work to move constantly toward this bar. This unfortunate process doesn't allow those with other learning styles and cognitive processes to feel accepted or normal. Many people like myself were built with hyperactive mental processing and out-of-the-box thinking from a young age. When you are required to be a part of these systems that push you to fit into the "norm," it makes it very easy to see that you are built differently. This can create scar tissue from a young age that can last throughout your entire life if you don't acknowledge your past experiences and connect with the fact that you are not meant to compete with others but rather to become the best version of yourself possible.

These core expectations and comparisons to others follow many of you through college and well into your business journey. The model is designed for competition with and comparison to others rather than developing you to become the best version of who you are. You might develop a mindset of constant expectation from others or comparisons to other people. This follows you deep into your adult life, career, finances, and many other areas. Unfortunately, the cycle continues in many people's lives. It's a difficult issue to contain, creating further problems that can even affect dating and marriage.

You have to take a step back and connect with those moments, with those voices and the rudimentary foundations that have been ingrained in you. You need to work to break away so that you can cut out the mental holdbacks, insecurities, or fears that may have come from this being a part of your life. This comparison or competition mentality and the bar set by the masses or in your childhood will not allow you to become the greatest version of yourself.

To become an entrepreneur and a highly motivated individual dedicated to your success, you have to break out of the norm. Expectations and comparisons keep people at the same bar or at the same level as others. *Your life needs to be different.* You need to break away from the patterns that have been ingrained in you, the expectations that have been placed on you, and the comparisons that are constantly pushed at you. The comparison tools in your life are your lighthouse, your greatness, and the future you are going after. Your daily steps and actions should be based on your capabilities and the hunger deep inside of you. Your comparison and competition should always be based on showing up as a better version of yourself than what showed up the day before. The drive and hunger that you use as fuel should be focused on greater results and based upon who you are.

Discover the Shining Lights, Not Competitors

There are people around you, on social media, or well-known individuals to whom you might find yourself drawn to compare yourself. Maybe you envy the outcomes they achieved. There will always be people who become part of your internal or external competition. It doesn't matter your successes or where you are in your business or career. You have to fight against this mindset and take a step back. Learn more about their journey and connect to them as shining lights or examples in your life, but don't focus on wishing for and wanting their results or expecting that you will be able to achieve their greatness. You are living a different life with a different story, and you will have your own outcome, not theirs.

As you look at each person and their results, focus on their journey rather than wishing for their outcome. Take time to learn about their struggles, what they had to overcome, who they are, and what they became despite their hardships. These individuals should inspire you to never quit and always go after your goals despite anything you face. These people should demonstrate that there is no success without struggle and that only the relentless will be rewarded for their greatest success.

Someone I look up to and have spent some time learning more about is actor and professional wrestler Dwayne "The Rock" Johnson. He has had massive success, but it was only achieved through a journey of hardships, struggles, and the relentless pursuit of his goals. He states, "Success isn't always about greatness. It's about consistency. Consistent hard work leads to success. Greatness will come."

The shift in your mindset from viewing these individuals as competition to seeing them as examples opens you to success that's based upon you. This allows you to not only look at the glory of what they became and what they have but also learn from their process and journey. With this shift in mindset, you can focus on their entire story and look at all the difficulties they encountered on their road to success. Yes, you can appreciate the peak of their life or the climax of their story, but now you can also connect to their entire life and acknowledge that these people are not your competitors.

You are on your own journey, writing your own story. To be able to work through all of your challenges, hardships, and difficulties, it's vital to channel every example and shining light that you can connect with. These examples are never your competition. They are proof that despite adversity, hardship, and getting your face kicked in on occasion, you can still get up and make sure that you show up as the best possible version of yourself.

It might seem like a tangent, but I want to caution you about jealousy and envy, and I believe it's crucial to address the topic here. I have seen many go down the slippery slope of jealousy and waste valuable time that they could have used to develop, grow, and chase after their own lighthouse. The mentality surrounding this type of rivalry can become destructive and cause a complete derailment from your journey. Remember that you are on your own road. You are owning your own life. You are writing your own future. If somebody else has already hit success or achieved their greatness, it doesn't affect your ability to do the same. They do not have what you deserve. They do not have what is yours. They do not have what you are chasing. So, jealousy is not what is eating you.

Being envious is based upon resentment or a desire to have someone else's possessions, success, achievements, or status. If you allow yourself to live in envy, it will eat you alive. The best version of who you are and what you're trying to achieve cannot exist if you live in envy. Allowing yourself to focus on only the positives of other people's stories, not looking at the roads they've had to travel to achieve those milestones, and being envious of their achievements creates a deep-rooted darkness inside you. Living with an envious mindset leaves you thinking there's not enough success, possessions, accomplishments, or status for everyone. *Realize that your success—or anyone else's—does not come at someone else's expense.* Other people don't have to fail for you to succeed. Your winning doesn't have to mean there are losers. Remember—there are no competitors, only the prior version of yourself. When you feel envious of another person's success, dig into their story and get a full understanding of how hard the road toward their success has been.

In this process, focus on the grit, determination, and hardships within the success stories around you. Focus on admiring who the people are and how they showed up as the best version of themselves every day to achieve the success that they now have. Focusing on competition and allowing envy to fester can lead down a road of distraction, and for some, it may even result in their destruction. The transition to appreciating these shining lights and examples will serve to encourage you on your hard roads. You have to look at your story, your life, your future, and the lighthouse you are chasing and keep focused on competing with only yourself.

No Outside Competitors

The idea of having no outside competitors might sound absolutely ridiculous to you, and I understand that there are moments when healthy competition can help improve a specific performance or result. This is not the case when it comes to the global aspect of life and your journey, goals, achievements, and success. The derailment seen with driven, motivated, and hungry individuals is most often due to a lack of focus, and too many times, this creates a lack of substantial results. You are living your life, not anyone else's. You have your own skills and abilities, not theirs. So why, then, are you competing with them? The competition mentality has many destructive aspects, but the core issue is that you are living *your* life, have *your* driving forces, and are chasing *your* lighthouse, so you cannot compete with anyone else. Others are driving on a different racetrack and chasing a different lighthouse. Competing with others moving in their own direction will constantly derail you. Your lighthouse will become foggy with the distractions of other people's goals and ambitions.

The track other people are running on is built based on their future, desired outcome, and greatest level of importance, not yours. Their vehicle is built for their particular race and is for their utilization, not yours. You can't have a monster truck competing on the same track as a dragster. Every vehicle is built for a different track, and the same is true for each of us.

In working through this process, you have to determine who you are and what your lighthouse is to identify the track you're running on. Your vehicle and another's can both be very powerful, built to excel and succeed in their own races. But always remember that your vehicle is built for a different intended purpose, skill set, strengths, best utilizations, and a different goal.

You have your own driving forces, your own lighthouse, your own purpose, your own skill sets, and a different life that you are living.

No one has the exact background, upbringing, experiences, cognitive processing, and mental wiring as you. No one is on your track with the history of where you've been and who you've been built to be. No one utilizes the same fuel that pushes you hard in your future direction. No one is pushing for your purpose. No one is living your life. And no one should be your competition. The only true competition is who you are versus who you need to be to achieve your desired outcome and greatest success.

You have to fully connect with who you are and work through the process in Chapter 5. Get clarity on who you can become and the best version of yourself that you're capable of. Learn to leverage your experiences, backgrounds, hurt, challenges, and difficulties to become the unstoppable force you were meant to be. You are building the exact machine needed for your race, and you have to decide whether you will invest the time and effort required to develop and maximize your abilities to handle your race and the track in front of you. You set the lighthouse in your life. What are the goals? What is the greatest version of you that you want and expect to show up?

This competition in your life should be focused only on how you show up each day versus the version of you that you are striving to be. You are the only one running your race, and it requires you to tap into the new version of you that will only show up once you set your mind to achieve your lighthouse and reach your better future. Your competition needs to be with the version of you that you allowed to show up yesterday. You have to outperform who you have let yourself be in the past and show up with new clarity, vision, drive and a new lighthouse.

Compete with the version of you that would let you fall back in your suck rather than chase after the greatness you're capable of achieving. The future you are chasing is in front of you and requires you to be dedicated to the goals and life that you are hungry to build. Don't let the distraction of competing with others derail your future. Instead, stay focused on the race you have entered with the vehicle that you have built.

CHAPTER 9

Foundation for Momentum

My lungs felt as if they were on fire. I was gasping for air and struggling to keep focused as we stood without any masks in a completely sealed chamber filled with tear gas. My face was draining from every orifice as I prepared to go through the gauntlet and shooter takedown building clearing. I sat in my thoughts for what seemed hours, but it was truly only minutes, contemplating my decision to take on the challenge of this specialized SWAT (special weapons and tactics) training.

When they opened the door to the chamber, I was greeted by ten aggressive SWAT training officers. I was required to fight through them while being pepper-sprayed to get to my equipment and then push toward a building that I had to clear for an active shooter. I fought through constant coughing, fluid draining from my face, physical exhaustion, and bleeding from the fight and trusted all the training I'd had to guide me through each step of the process.

This brutal activity repeated itself three times, one for each type of tear gas that's frequently used—CN, CS, and OC. This exercise seemed excessive to many—like it was some type of cruel and unusual torture—but I knew it was preparation for potential future situations. Some trainees quit, some fell apart under pressure, and some were transported to the hospital, but I dug deep into the process and welcomed the suffering because I knew that the harder I pushed myself in training, the more prepared I would be for anything I might face.

After the punishment of this training examination, the officers still standing were called to compete in a game of SWAT ball. Yes, it's just as aggressive as it sounds and is intended to push us all to our physical limits and test our cardio capabilities after we have been to hell and back.

This SWAT training I signed up for was one of the most advanced and severe and was known for its rough tactics. I understood that there was a specific purpose for every training and mission—even the SWAT ball that they required us to participate in. It was all part of the process of equipping me with the necessary tools and training to ensure I had the foundation necessary to confront any hardships I would encounter as a SWAT officer. There were no shortcuts, "jimmy rigs," or fake-it-till-you-make-it angles that could prepare me and get me ready to take on what I would need to do in the next leg of my journey as a SWAT officer. The development of this foundation was required to ensure that I would be ready to manage what was to come in my career. The same is true in your life. This book has covered a lot of ground that, if utilized and implemented, will be the core of the foundation that is necessary for you to chase after your future and the greatest version of yourself.

There are no shortcuts. *There is no way to achieve the type of success you are working to achieve without doing the required work.* The momentum you want, need, and drive after in your life must be built on a solid foundation. I have designed this book to take you through all the foundation-building that will create the catalyst for your future success. This foundation is needed to build the momentum required to achieve your lighthouse and the life you are driven and motivated to have.

Your Lighthouse Is Now Clear

The more clearly you can define your lighthouse, the harder you can charge toward your future. Building this momentum comes through daily successes and movements toward the vision of what you are built to be and what you aim to accomplish. When you have clearly identified your goals, what you're going after, and the greatness you're striving to become, all daily processes and actions should move you in that direction.

Using the driving forces and fuel you have channeled, you'll put actions in place day after day to move you toward the future you're chasing. If your lighthouse is not clearly defined, then the results of your daily actions won't be focused in a singular direction. If you don't have a clear picture of the greatest version of yourself and the success that you're built to achieve, how can you get focused results? If you've not done the work to clearly identify your lighthouse and hyperfocus on who you are and what you can become, you need to revisit Chapters 5 and 6 and do the required work.

You're hurting yourself and limiting your future by not fully connecting to the principles laid out in this book. The roadmap is in front of you. Break down your goals and delineate your desired successes. Create a definition of the potential greatness that you can and will achieve. Participation is required—too many want to talk about the success they're hungry for and the goals they'd like to achieve, but only a few are willing to do the work required to actually become the greatest version of themselves and find their true success.

It's incredible to look at different entrepreneurs and the outcome of their hard work and dedication. I have seen many who clearly identified their lighthouse, leveraged their hunger, drive, ambition, and hyperfocused on their precisely defined goals, made strides toward success, and hit achievements that the prior version of them would never have imagined possible. Their dedication to achieving results—and how quickly it can happen—is nothing shy of impressive. When you're hungry, driven, and motivated, clarifying the future you're chasing enables you to concentrate all your energy and abilities in one direction. *Your lighthouse is the guiding light for every step you take on your journey.* With this being clear and well-defined in your life, you can stop the pinball approach filled with shiny objects and disruptions and be fully dedicated to your desired outcome.

A Clear Vision of Your Suck

With your lighthouse and the vision of who you are capable of becoming in front of you, the identification of your suck becomes overwhelmingly clear. *Your suck is anything keeping you from getting to your lighthouse and becoming the greatest version of yourself.* Take the time to update, define and clarify what your suck looks like so you know when you're falling back into it or making decisions that will lead you in the wrong direction. Be aware of any daily pitfalls or habits that threaten to drive you back toward your suck and keep you from your lighthouse.

Almost everyone desires a better life and wants some form of success, but only those who are driven, dedicated, and hungry will actually achieve the results they're chasing. Rather than doing the work and being dedicated to their lighthouse, many will settle into their complacency or comfort and find themselves in a version of their suck. Others will find themselves stuck in their suck because of a lack of focus and an unwillingness to lay the proper foundation and do the required work. Reflect on your own life and determine where your holdbacks are. Distinguish between the paths that lead back to your suck and those you must walk to reach your most outstanding results. Your suck should be more clear than ever and part of the fuel that you channel to reach your lighthouse and never allow yourself to move back into your suck.

Fears and Insecurities

You cannot let the enticement of comfort, ease, and security keep you from chasing your greatness and success. Taking action toward your future will require seasons of extreme growth, hard decisions, and fears that need to be conquered. Fear is meant to be a pause point where you identify the risk and then decide to either fall back or charge forward. Fear will always be a part of every growth process you put yourself through. It should never cripple you or keep you from taking the right leap. Fear is a barrier and a filter that separates those who succeed from those who live in complacency.

As you're working through this process in your life, you will face fear. Those fears will come from different aspects of your past, your situation, and even who you are. You will only succeed by charging forward despite your fears and taking action. Yes, it's important to identify risks so you can make educated and wise decisions, but you cannot let your fear be the crippling point of your momentum. The holdbacks at your core and the fear that you're allowing yourself to cater to need to be identified and addressed, and you must be resolved to take action despite your fears and push to chase your greatness.

The truth about fear is that it is often coupled with or even caused by insecurities in your life. To address the fears holding you back, you must identify and work through your insecurities. This type of self-doubt has no place in the greatness that you are built for and will only hold you back from who you are called to be. You must take the time to work through each of them and find out why they exist. You have lived with these insecurities and have taken some action despite them, but where do they come from? Acknowledge the hardships in your past that magnify and even create self-doubt.

Every insecurity is a holdback and resistance to the momentum you're building. Imagine trying to race with a parachute attached to your vehicle—it will slow down and stunt the vehicle's performance. Similarly, your insecurities have the potential to slow your progress and impede the momentum of your journey. By identifying your insecurities, understanding their origins, and addressing their core aspects, you can embark on a healing process, allowing you to drive forward with less resistance.

A big part of this process in your life is determining the actions you need to take to help grow and develop yourself and minimize the triggers and the root of these insecurities. For some, it might be weight loss or strength training. For others, it might be taking a class on public speaking. It could also be some kind of specialized training or license. Whatever the case may be in your life, you have to do the work to become more confident mentally and know you are built to be who and what you are chasing. You cannot let insecurities keep you from your lighthouse, and in many cases, it's not just about doing the work to cope with the insecurities mentally. There are core actions you need to take to make sure that you're always bettering yourself and minimizing the driving factors behind your insecurities.

There are too many people who never find success or achieve their full potential because they always cater to their insecurities rather than countering and resolving them. After you take the time to identify where these are in your life, you have to determine where they stem from. Some of them can be worked through mentally or with a therapist, but others are resolved only by taking action to overcome them.

Many of the insecurities that I see holding back entrepreneurs can be counterbalanced and resolved by dedicated action and effort. Even in dealing with some of my own, I have to push to identify the actions I can take that will resolve or minimize them so that they don't become holdbacks. People who are insecure about their weight or their physique have to dedicate themselves to the counterbalance, which is trimming a few pounds or adding in a strength-training regimen. I understand that this counterbalance might not fix the deep-rooted core issues, but it will definitely give your confidence a boost and minimize the effects of insecurity on your life.

Other examples of insecurities that I have seen frequently in entrepreneurs include a lack of business knowledge, professional communication skills, formal education, public speaking ability, and industry experience. There are ways that you can work to counterbalance each one. They aren't overnight fixes, but with dedication and the right process, you can put steps in place to resolve and even remove these from your life.

You have to take the inventory and connect with the insecurities and fears that are a part of your holdbacks. Don't just accept them and dodge any activities that magnify them, but rather meet them head-on. Where do fears and insecurities sit in your life, and what work do you need to do to build a more solid foundation?

The Ownership You Are Taking

A vital part of the foundation for the momentum in your life is being honest with yourself about why you have been in your suck or have not been moving toward your lighthouse. There are actions in your life, or a lack of actions, that are keeping you in your suck versus allowing you to achieve your lighthouse. As former Navy SEAL officer Jocko Willink stated in his book *Extreme Ownership*, "Implementing extreme ownership requires checking your ego and operating with a high degree of humility, admitting mistakes, taking ownership, and developing a plan to overcome challenges."

In your life, you have to take extreme ownership and adopt the humility needed to admit your mistakes and take ownership of your actions. Look at everything that is moving you away from or keeping you in your suck.

As a quick reality check:
- What actions have you taken while reading or listening to this book?
- Have you done the work that I have laid out in each chapter?
- Have you gone to the resources page for more support and information?

- Have you taken any action steps while going through this book?

When asked what the key to success is, Dwayne Johnson answered, "The key is, there is no key. Be humble, hungry, and the hardest worker in the room." In Chapter 10, we will dig deeper into taking ownership of who you are and what you have done, but the foundations required for this are discussed throughout this book. You need to confront the truth: Are you genuinely prepared for action and forward progress, or are you simply seeking another book that serves as a cheerleader or offers a fleeting feel-good moment? There's a major difference between those ready for their future success and those who just talk about what they want to become. Your future is knocking, but your reality might be your holdback from answering.

In this process, you have to accept honesty and the truth about your life, your actions, and who you have allowed yourself to show up as. There is a brutal unraveling and openness that you have to have about some internal issues and the holdbacks that are keeping you from your greatness. It's not easy to connect with and open up about the hardships you have faced in your life, but you have to be honest and real about doing the work to build the foundation required. *Your future is begging you to do what is necessary to get you out of your own way to become your greatest self and achieve your lighthouse.* There are no shortcuts, and it will require extreme ownership of who you are, what is holding you back, and where your failures have been. The first step is to decide whether you're willing to do the work required to lay the foundation needed to be the catalyst for your forever.

Document and Detail

There's a massive gap between your suck and your lighthouse. *How you take action and handle this next phase of your life will determine whether you achieve your lighthouse or fall back toward your suck.* It is absolutely vital for you to connect with, document, and detail where you are running from and where you are running to. I have a saying—if it's not written, it didn't happen. This principle can be applied to many aspects of life. When it comes to your goals, future, skill sets, hunger, and everything else that will drive you to the best version of yourself, it should all be documented and detailed to hold you accountable.

The same is true for everything that allows you to fall back into the more complacent, settled, or held-back version of you. You have the suck on one side and the lighthouse on the other, so having a clear understanding of your direction of travel is important—which one is in front of you and which one needs to remain behind you? Detailing and documenting this and leaving yourself reminders of why you're never going back to your suck will keep you focused on your lighthouse. Write down the warning signs for the distractions, disruptions, and internal holdbacks that might cause your derailment. Always remember why you are moving forward toward your lighthouse.

Go back to your driving forces and the details of why you are hungry, driven, and motivated to chase after your goals and ambitions. Create videos, audio recordings, notes, and even signs to put on your walls that detail out the fuel that is pushing you forward so you never allow yourself to live in, be comfortable in, or move toward your suck. Whether it's for family members, people around you, for a better future, for a legacy, or whatever, send yourself videos or reminders. It's important to remember why you never want to allow yourself to fall into your suck and need to always show up every day as the person who is going to chase after your lighthouse.

As you walk through this, you will need plenty of fuel. Going back to Chapter 4, you should have written down the details of all your driving forces, all the fuel that ignites the fire in you that drives you to achieve your lighthouse. Work through this process on a daily basis. Break down and confront the lens issues you face and how they may derail your progress. Detail out the potential barriers that stem from your lens issues and remind yourself why they are not truths but rather reflections of your past and pain—mere obstacles in your life. Document, detail, and provide yourself reminders that these holdbacks do not define who you are. Instead, they are hurdles you must overcome on your journey toward your best self.

Expect and Accept From Yourself

The fundamental truth for you at this very moment is that only you can find success, hit your goals, and achieve the results you expect and accept from yourself. You can take in all the principles, get the roadmaps, and hear all the inspiring stories, but you have to lay the foundation for what you are going to require of yourself. Are you going to allow yourself to live in your suck, or do you expect and require greatness from yourself? You have to set expectations, goals, and boundaries for what is allowable and acceptable in your life. It will not come down to what you want your life to become but rather what you will require of yourself on the journey to achieve your desired results.

Your life will have results, but those results will be influenced by the expectations you set for yourself, what you accept from yourself on your journey, and the actions you require of yourself. You need to connect with the fact that everyone wants success, but only those willing to chase hard after it, pushing past comfort, security, complacencies, fears, and insecurities, will ever achieve it. Your life is not about what you want, and it's not just about the goals that you set. It's about the actions you require of yourself. You have to lay the foundation of what you are going to expect and accept from yourself to gain momentum toward your lighthouse.

Foundation for Your Momentum

This foundation that you're building will be the groundwork for the momentum required to achieve your greatest results and part of the launchpad toward your success. As you develop and secure the infrastructure that will be the catalyst for your future, it's important to have guidance and accountability to ensure that you are working through the required core elements. The process and development of these core aspects and details of what you will use to achieve the greatest results require attention and focus. A good system of checks and balances, as well as direct guidance through the process, is strongly recommended to make sure you're not limiting yourself and are connecting fully to your holdbacks, roadblocks, and your greatest potential. You need clarity on your direction and confidence in the foundation that has been laid. Working with the right mentor, coach, or team can help you fast-track toward your success and ensure you are chasing in a direction that will get you to your greatest results. You will be tired, and you will have missteps, but having the right team in your corner will keep you from straying toward the easier paths and dedicated to the actions required to achieve your lighthouse.

You need a team or a coach to keep you focused in your moments of weakness when that comfort is so easy to fall back into. These people can't be people who are comfortable in their suck. They can't be people who allow their fears and insecurities to control their future and destiny. They need to understand what it's like to be chasing greatness and what it takes to pull out the best version of you and keep you focused on your lighthouse. The team around you must have proven success and always be driven to achieve a better future for themselves. They must be able to advise on your situation without any ambition for themselves. The resources page I have provided gives more guidance on how to identify and choose the right coach for you. It also gives information on additional support that my team offers for your journey.

The road to your lighthouse requires you to be dedicated to greatness. As you drive forward and build momentum in your life to take action toward your future, it is absolutely vital to ensure that your foundation is solid. Your dedication to success and achieving greatness requires you to channel and focus your attention on the right foundational elements, as this will serve as the launchpad toward your future. Your ability to improve each day and strive for greatness relies on the work you've done to create the catalyst for your greatest success.

CHAPTER 10

Suck Less, Do Better Every Day

"Don't wish it was easier, wish you were better. Don't wish for less problems, wish for more skills. Don't wish for less challenge, wish for more wisdom." – Jim Rohn

The story of your life and your future is waiting on *you*. This book is a complete guide that will be the catalyst you need if you follow the process. I have used the strategies within this book to go from being almost bankrupt to becoming a multi-millionaire in less than ten years. Now faced with the opportunity to retire, I choose to continue to chase the greatest version I am capable of to have the biggest impact.

Growing up, I wasn't the smartest person in the room and was never on the "most likely to succeed" list. However, I was driven, hungry, and motivated to find success despite all odds, and I'm still charging hard after the future version of myself that I know I can become. Along my journey, I recognized the importance of fully connecting with all the pain, difficulties, hardships and process to ensure that when I achieved success I could support others on their journey.

Your next steps will determine whether you make it or break it. You now know how you can shape the trajectory of your life and who you become. If you finish this book but fail to do the work, neglect to take the necessary steps, and continue making excuses for your results, you'll end up with another failure on your list. Jim Rohn expressed his feelings on this matter: "Don't wish it was easier, wish you were better. Don't wish for fewer problems—wish for more skills. Don't wish for less challenge—wish for more wisdom." This book will not solve all your problems, but it can be the catalyst to get you on the right path toward your lighthouse and get you out of your own way. Working through this book and the principles laid out inside is where the excuses in your life end. If you fail, it will be your fault.

This Is Where Your Excuses End

You can't settle for *good* when you're called to be *great*. You can't work through this book and not take action. You now have the formula and the process to identify what you're running from, the driving forces in your life, who you are built to be, and what you're chasing, as well as how to eliminate the excuses and conquer the holdbacks. Before this, you may have been moving through your journey without the right guidance and direction to help you find the success you've been discussing, dreaming about, and even faking.

That excuse is now completely gone.

This book was not written just to get you hyped up and motivated to take action. It's an entire manual on how to get you to great success by taking the right actions and following the right processes in your life. I developed this book and provided additional resources to ensure that you will have no excuses when you finish this last chapter. When you remove holdbacks, ignite your driving forces, and acknowledge your broken lenses, you will have a clear lens through which you can view your lighthouse.

Focused attention and dedicated actions will allow you to achieve the result you're chasing. The longer you delay taking the right actions, the more likely you are to fall back into your suck rather than achieve your lighthouse. The core aspects and foundations in this book have changed my life and the lives of many, but each one of us had something in common—dedication to action. If you're here in the final chapter and haven't yet done the work I've covered in the book, then I would strongly encourage you to take a step back and do it. If you don't do the work, it's clear where the issues are in your life. You might be one of those people who always has an excuse for why you don't succeed, don't get the growth you want, or don't get the success that you're chasing. If you take an inventory of your past, it's probably easy to see that there was a lot of talk, a lot of listening, a lot of reading, and attempted learning. But the truth is that there has to be application and action. Learning new information—and planning—becomes null and void if you don't take action.

Your failure from this point on is completely on you. You can't say that no one gave you a roadmap, no one broke down the process, and no one cared enough to provide the secret to success. This book was written after reverse-engineering how I became extremely successful and overcame all odds. This is how I continue to move forward and achieve great results despite the hardships and difficulties I have faced. These principles extend beyond my own life—I have worked with many entrepreneurs, guiding them through this exact process and witnessing the greatness they achieved. I have seen them break free from cycles of insanity to thrive and attain the results they're chasing. Your future demands that you put an end to excuses and take the right actions to achieve success.

Clarity Provides Vision, Vision Gives Direction, and Participation Is Required

Clarity in your life is paramount and should be escalated to the top of your priority list. Development of the fundamental process discussed in this book will help you gain clarity about who you are, what you're built for, and what you're chasing. You have to do the work laid out in each chapter and directly apply these concepts and theories to your life, your history, your future, and your success. The discovery of your lighthouse will be one of the greatest and most invigorating moments you can ever have. Fully understanding what you're chasing and having a vision of what you are built to accomplish creates clarity for your journey's path.

Clarifying who you are called to become and built to be now provides your long-term vision of what you have to chase after. You are left with the truth that participation in your life is absolutely mandatory, and action is required. Your participation in the race toward your lighthouse is the only way for you to find your greatest success. Your suck must remain in your rearview mirror as you do the daily work to move toward your lighthouse. At the end of your life, will you be satisfied with a participation trophy? Or will you go hard after success and achievement to gain the greatest reward by becoming the best and most unstoppable version of yourself? Your future requires you to gain clarity, find your clear vision, and then put the action steps in place that will lead you down the path to greatness.

Take Ownership of Who You Are

Take inventory of what you have done to grow, develop, and better yourself to achieve success. Look at your past to see where you've shown up and conquered the challenges that you faced. Look at your accomplishments and decide if this is the greatest level of achievement that you are built for. When taking inventory, you must also identify your failures and missteps. How did you learn from those? How can you adapt? How do you ensure you don't fall back into the same habits or the same trap? You must eliminate all the excuses that you've made for your past mistakes and instead identify weaknesses, patterns, bad habits, and internal holdbacks that you need to correct.

Understand that there's always something to learn despite the level of fault you feel you may have. Jocko Willink states, "Realistic assessment, acknowledgment of failure, and ownership of the problem were key to developing a plan to improve performance and ultimately win." Look back at your life. What opportunities are there that you failed to learn from, take ownership of, and grow through the experiences? The easy road is to shift the blame for your current reality, past mistakes, or past issues in your life. But there isn't a scoreboard for positive points earned and mistakes or bad decisions ignored. You can't glorify your wins and minimize your failures. The converse is also true—you can't beat yourself up for all your failures and ignore all your accomplishments. You have to look at it all through a realistic lens and focus on learning, developing, growing, and strengthening yourself to build a better future.

The level of ownership required for you to achieve the goals that you set for yourself and the success you're chasing can be painful. Work through the following questions with openness and true ownership of where you are in your journey:

- Are your past efforts and actions enough to get you the results you want in your life?
- Have you shown up in a way that will allow you to hit your goals?
- Have you failed because you've given up or taken the easy road?
- Is the level of effort that you have put toward your future going to be enough to achieve the greatest version of your success?
- What excuses have you used to give up or to take the easy way out?
- What part of your life do you need to step back and take ownership of?
- What roadblocks might you be creating for your future?
- Are you going to take the required actions moving forward, or will you settle for life's participation trophy?

Remember, you can never settle for *good* because you are called to be *great*. Yes, there will be hurdles, difficulties, and challenges in your path, but you alone have the authorship of your story and how your life will be read. You have to make sure to identify the areas of difficulty and hardship you have created, magnified, or failed to resolve. There's always an opportunity to learn. *The past has the lessons that you can leverage to change the course of your future.*

Hurt and Difficulties of the Past

As you sit and reflect on different situations and your past circumstances to connect with the learning and growth that can be uncovered, you are also faced with the hurt and difficulties laced throughout your journey. You must be aware that these things are only a part of your story and do not define who you are or your future. Don't use them as an excuse to not show up as who you are built to be and go hard after your future. The past, hurt, and difficulties need to be filtered so you can determine what can be used as fuel to move you forward. Sitting and soaking in your hurt and licking your wounds will never be a catalyst or create momentum toward your future. *Stop making excuses for your lack of action or results by focusing on what other people have done to you, how life is not fair, or how the world has wronged you.*

I can already hear it from those of you who soak in the past and make excuses. "Nate, you don't understand. My life has been this, or I have been through that." I hope this is not you, as these excuses are nothing but barriers to your future that you're allowing to get in your way. I understand that you have a story, and it could be riddled with hurt, trauma, and hardships. There have also been major struggles and hardships in my life that would break the spirit of most people.

However, I have set my mind and heart to relentlessly chase who I am called to be and what I am called to accomplish. I do this not only to push hard toward my lighthouse but also to impact the lives of others on my journey. I am not here to pity you for your life circumstances but rather to call you to conquer what is in front of you. Life will bring formidable challenges, and each of us will encounter roadblocks and difficulties. Your relentless spirit and the grit deep inside you will allow you to overcome those struggles and succeed.

Author and educator Booker T. Washington expresses the measure of success this way: "Success is to be measured not so much by the position that one has reached in life as by the obstacles which he has overcome." All these pain points, difficulties, hardships, roadblocks, and seemingly impossible giants you've had to face are not the end of your story. They give you the opportunity to write a story that will have an impact on those who are going through similar situations. Your story can be a beacon of light in their darkness and an example of true success. Your story should prove that you can overcome, conquer, and take on anything in your path to achieve greatness.

The road to your greatest success is not exempt from hardship, hurt, and pain, but it will be even sweeter when you know that you have fought through every storm on the way. The scars you acquire on your journey serve as proof that you've fought to overcome what once seemed impossible. You're the author of your own story, and you have the power to choose how you'll respond and what the outcome will be. Embrace the challenges you've faced and transform those past experiences into an unstoppable force. Refuse to let anything hinder you from achieving the greatness you're destined for.

Entitlement is for the Complacent and Settled

A major holdback evident in the lives of many individuals is entitlement. By this point, I'm sure you know my opinion on this success killer. You cannot wait for anyone or anything to provide a future for you. No one else can write your story, and no one else will save you. The greatest version of who you can become does not include anyone else doing the grinding or the hard work for you. You must decide what you want your life to look like, the level of success you aim to achieve, and what your story will ultimately say. Will it reflect someone who is an unstoppable force, or will it depict someone who is entitled, complacent, and settled and allows their greatest abilities, opportunities, and potential to go to waste?

In the future, you will look at yourself in the mirror and either be satisfied with the results you have produced or ashamed of who you have allowed yourself to become. Jim Rohn explained this in a way that is undeniably true: "We must all suffer one of two things: the pain of discipline or the pain of regret." There are no handouts, no freebies, and no free rides that will get you to your lighthouse. You have to choose to go hard after life despite anything that comes.

Know that you are the hero of your own story, and no one is coming to rescue you. That hunger inside of you needs to turn into a focused drive toward the future and the lighthouse you're chasing. Never let a hint of entitlement creep into your mind or spirit, and never expect others to solve your problems. This will destroy your drive and progression toward the greatest version of you. Your future is in your hands, and the results you achieve depend on your efforts, actions, drive, and focus.

Show Up Daily

As you continue your journey, you must resolve to show up daily as who you are called to be. The decision is in front of you: Are you going to live as the person you are built to be or allow yourself to continue as the settled version of your past? I'm not asking what actions you will take each day, but rather, I am asking whether you have set your mind, heart, and spirit to show up each day as the best version of who you can be. Determination is required in each of our lives. There's a switch that needs to be flipped to transform from *who you have allowed yourself to be* to *who you are called to be*. You can read all the books on the market and take every developmental course available, but your momentum will be stifled until you resolve that the only option for your future is the most excellent version of who you can become.

This decision to show up daily as who you are called to be will require sacrifice, discipline, dedication, and a relentless mindset. You have to determine whether you're ready for the challenges, difficulties, and hardships on your road to greatness or whether you're going to crawl back to your comfort zone when the road gets tough. When you decide to become who you are called to be and dedicate yourself to showing up daily, your life will never look the same. Your life—focused and settled to achieve the version of who you are built to be and what you are capable of—should be charged with daily actions to gain focused momentum.

Momentum Through Daily Execution

The lighthouse you're chasing and the clear vision of who you are called to be is in the distance, and the steps you take each day move you down the pathway of your journey. You can see the goals, ambitions, greatness, and success that you have set as your lighthouse, but momentum is required to achieve those results. Having focus gives you the direction and groundwork needed to chase hard after your lighthouse. Your momentum is found only through the execution of the daily habits required to move in the right direction. The road is not an easy one and will require discipline and dedication during the hard times. As President Theodore Roosevelt once said, "With self-discipline, most anything is possible."

Your daily actions are either going to drive you toward your lighthouse or allow you to fall back into your suck. You have to be dedicated each and every day to moving the needle of your life forward toward your lighthouse and focusing on the long-term outcome of who you want to become. Author and speaker James Clear, in his book *Atomic Habits,* states, "Making a choice that is 1 percent worse seems insignificant at the moment. But over the span of moments that make up a lifetime, these choices determine the difference between who you are and who you could be. Success is a production of daily habits, not once-in-a-lifetime transformations."

There are no magical buttons to press, pills to take, or overnight fixes for transformations you want to make in your life. The only way to your success is by taking the actions required to achieve it. I have a saying in business: "If it's easy, it's not your answer." Easy businesses, easy careers, easy financial goals, and an easy life won't get you the results you're striving for. So why are you looking for the easy road to get you where you want to be? There is a process and daily work that is required. If you want to succeed beyond the norm, then you have to be willing to work beyond the norm. This is not about working endless hours but rather about having a focused mission and efforts dedicated to that mission. A compounding effect will occur when you choose to focus on daily actions that allow you to grow and take strides toward your lighthouse.

The momentum you build with your daily efforts becomes a part of the fuel that keeps you moving toward your goals, dreams, and the best version of yourself. You must show up daily, make sure your actions are aligned with your mission, and be focused on achieving your goals, ambitions, and most extraordinary future. There will be days when you can focus on incremental adjustments that will compound toward your future, but there will also be moments that are going to require you to make drastic changes and take swift action. You have to be confident in the lighthouse that you are setting for your future and have a solid understanding of who you are meant to be. Then, show up each day with the dedication and determination required to push forward and build on the momentum from your prior efforts. Your level of future success and the achievements available to you will be discovered through showing up daily, driving hard toward who you are built to be, and discovering the momentum you can build on your journey.

Inventory of Actions

Brutal honesty is required when looking at your life and how you have shown up. You have to take inventory of your actions and the level of momentum each one brings toward chasing your success. Detail out all the actions that you have attempted, utilized, and failed at, and even some that you haven't tried. Rank them one through ten, with one being the lowest amount of momentum and ten being the highest. The resources page at the end of the book has more information on this to assist you. This is not a quick exercise and not something you can do in just a few minutes. It's an analysis of what your actions were and how they have or will impact movement toward your lighthouse. These actions and details don't have to be extravagant. Start with the simple items and build from there.

In this same process, it's important to also detail out actions or habits that are holding you back or driving you toward your suck. Use the same ranking system, one to ten, with one being the lowest amount of holdback and ten being the highest. This must be done down to the simplest distractions and actions that keep you from taking the right steps or distract you from growth and development. Remember that it doesn't have to be a bad thing to be a holdback. There are things in life that might be neutral, but if there is excessive time spent in these areas, it could be holding you back from spending that time on something that can build momentum. Gaming, social media, reading novels, and even watching movies might not be bad if you do them in moderation, but to those who are driven to achieve a better future, they can become distractions or holdbacks.

Major disclaimer: *I never feel that family and core relationships should be sacrificed to achieve results.*

People are a major part of the driving forces within many of us, and I wouldn't want you to do anything to damage your family or the core relationships in your life. This is a deep subject that would take too many pages to dig into fully, but I felt it necessary to mention it to ensure you don't go to the extreme.

As you review your list of actions that build momentum, compare them to the lighthouse and goals you have set for yourself. Decide whether these actions will be the right foundation on which to build your future and whether they can get you to your lighthouse. There are often gaps in the foundation and actions missing from the list that need to be included. It's just like learning how to play an instrument. There are principles that you must study and learn to fully develop into the best musician possible. Skipping these rudiments doesn't mean you won't be able to play music, but it will limit the level you'll reach as a musician. Your list must include the principles and actions necessary to build the foundation for your lighthouse. To get to the greatest version of you and achieve the greatest goals, the foundation is vital.

You probably know what's coming next, but I have to put it in here. You have to cut out the distractions, actions, and habits holding you back. You can't allow these to keep you from who you can become and what you are built to achieve. I'm not telling you not to live, not to have balance, and not to enjoy life, but I am telling you that you need to set your goals and chase hard after them. This requires sacrifice, and only the willing, driven, and focused will be determined enough to remove the holdbacks and push full force into their future.

This is a tough process for many and can bring up a reality that isn't always pleasant to face, but the truth that's uncovered can be great leverage for your future. Information and knowledge are only valuable to those who take action. The inventory process isn't just a one-time thing. It's ongoing through the different stages of your journey. You will have to constantly learn, develop, grow, and adjust to achieve your goals and your greatest success. Look at the momentum that you're gaining on a daily basis and see if it's going to be enough to get you the results you're hungry for.

The *future you* depends on the *current you* to chase the goals and ambitions you have set for yourself. The future version of you is relying on this very moment—and every day after—for you to keep the focus, the dedication, and the promises that you have made to yourself. You will only achieve your greatest results by taking the right action steps each and every day.

Every Day Is Your Day to Suck Less, Do Better

The decision at this crossroads is yours alone. No one else can make it for you. What version of you will you take into every day going forward? The complacent, settled, comfort-seeking, easy-road-chasing and excuse-making version, or the relentless, hungry, dedicated, challenge-facing, risk-taking, reality-checking, and always adapting version? Have you determined how you will show up each day to push hard toward your lighthouse? Being who you are called to be requires dedication. It requires approaching each day as a new opportunity to make progress toward the greatest version of yourself. You cannot waste the days in front of you. The best version of who you are needs to surface to keep the momentum moving toward your lighthouse.

Each day will require you to take ownership of your actions, direction, and future to make sure you never settle and are always making progress toward the future you're after. Dwayne Johnson said, "Success isn't always about greatness. It's about consistency. Consistent hard work leads to success. Greatness will come." You must show up and take action to get to your lighthouse with no excuses. Every movement each day must be purposeful. Remove distractions that could derail your progress. Dedicate yourself to your lighthouse and your future, as your success is yours alone to achieve. The greatness you have the potential to achieve lies ahead, and you must never settle for a lesser version of what you are called to be. Stay connected to your driving forces because this is the fuel that will keep you moving forward despite the roadblocks and difficulties you face.

Let go of yesterday's failures. Today is a new day to gain momentum toward your forever. Learn from your failures and celebrate your victories. Push hard into your strengths and live in your relentless spirit. Take steps toward the future with daily actions that will compound and get you to your lighthouse. You are not built to give up and crawl back to your suck. Easy roads and comfort will lead to failure. *Those hungry for success are willing to take on the daily challenge of pushing themselves to their greatest potential despite hardships.* As the author of your story, you are charged with the responsibility to turn any hardship or difficulties you face into a story of greatness. You have to show up and live the life you will be proud of for others to read. You must take the action required to make yourself great and achieve the lighthouse you set as your mission. You have to make the determination to suck less and do better to find the unstoppable you.

CONCLUSION

Live in Your Suck or Succeed

There are no more excuses because you now know too much. This book is a guide to help you work through everything holding you back from greatness. You have to take the time to do the work and put all these principles into action. This foundation will be your catalyst to greatness if you make the decision to travel the road to your lighthouse. If you have not already done the work in this book, you need to go back and work through each and every step of the process to build the foundation for your future.

You are in control of what this will look like in your life. You are the author of what you want the rest of your story to be. Don't hold back; find the road toward the greatest version of who you can become, and charge hard with an unstoppable mindset. Don't let your excuses, fears, or insecurities keep you from taking the right daily actions toward your success. You cannot settle on *good* because you are called to be *great*. You have to be relentless and dedicated to suck less and do better every day to conquer the difficulties, hardships, and obstacles that will be on the path to your greatest success.

These next steps on your journey and the actions you take after reading this book will be a major part of what defines the outcome of your life. I am sure you want and need to understand more about who you are, what you are built to become, and how to set the right lighthouse for your life. Because I'm dedicated to impacting your life, I won't leave you hanging. I have resources, programs, and coaching to help you continue this journey. Go to our free resources page—the link is at the end of this conclusion. There's information there about some other opportunities that I have for you. There is a major difference between those who take action and those who just want and wish. You have to decide which you are going to be. Jim Rohn stated, "You cannot change your destination overnight, but you can change your direction overnight." This is your time to decide the direction you are going to travel. Are you dedicated to ending your excuses and allowing for the rise of the unstoppable you?

Impact Others on Your Journey

This journey you are on and the process you're working through is a mountain that few choose to climb. Many stand on the sidelines, watching others and waiting for support and encouragement to take on their own journey. I challenge you to let your process and your journey be an encouragement to others around you and an impact on those you can reach. Be a part of other people's success stories and take others on this journey with you. Use your life as an example to shine as a light to others. Connect others to this book and the programs available on my resource page. Give them the gift of a future and success in their lives by telling your story and how this book was a part of your journey. Give them the gift of freedom to live the best version of who they can become by taking them through your journey and guiding them to where you discovered these principles. The greatest version of you isn't built only on your success. Life is about having an impact on the lives of others.

My Hope and Goals

I know that in my life, I have been through many challenges, difficulties, and hardships, and I've made the choice to never give up, never quit, and never take the easy roads of comfort and security that lead back to my suck. I made a promise to myself that I would always push beyond my comfort zone and chase hard to create an impact in the lives of as many people as I can. In constantly pushing myself forward, I've taken on many challenges that have extended my limits, and the writing of this book is a perfect example. Two years ago, I would have laughed at the thought of writing a book, and I would have let my fears, insecurities, and cracked lenses hold me back.

Through the process of always improving, growing, learning, and developing myself to become the best version of me, I have chosen to challenge my abilities in every way and am always dedicated to *Suck Less, Do Better*. Through this, I felt called to continue on my journey toward greatness by getting the processes and strategies laid out in a book that can have a massive impact for a low cost. My goal is to make a difference in the lives of millions of people by being one of the catalysts that move them toward greatness. My hope is that by being open about my hardships, experiences, and life lessons, you can connect with some or all of these and find inspiration to keep moving forward toward your lighthouse.

I am still a work in progress and never claim to have it all figured out. That is why the principle of suck less, do better is one that is never finished—there is *always* a better version of myself that I can become. I hope that your life will be changed by reading about how I got outside my comfort zone, chased hard toward my greatness, and tried (and still try) to live a life that is a light to those I can reach.

Get connected to the resources I have provided you, and keep me updated on your journey. I want to know more about where you are in your process. I want to hear about your results. I want to know that the road I'm chasing down has had an impact on your life. Tag me on social media—@IamNateGreen—and tell me about your journey. Use #SuckLessDoBetter to inspire others with your message and the future you are chasing. The greatest version of you is still yet to come. *Always suck less, do better.*

Resources Available

I understand that this book moves quickly and covers a lot of ground. In an effort to make a meaningful impact in your life and recognize that you may need some assistance along this journey, I am providing additional resources to support you. I challenge you to revisit each chapter and work through them a second time while using the checklists and resources I have made available for you. Dive deep into the tasks and reflect on who you are, ensuring that you extract all the valuable information from each chapter to build your foundation.

THANK YOU FOR READING MY BOOK!

DOWNLOAD YOUR FREE GIFTS

The free resources are available at the link below, or you can scan the QR Code for quick reference. This resources page has downloads, checklists, worksheets, and videos. You can learn more about the programs, coaching, and additional support I have available to help you through the process of how to get out of your suck and chase your lighthouse.

To Download Now, Visit:
www.SuckLessDoBetterBook.com/Resources

I appreciate your interest in my book and value your feedback as it helps me improve future versions of this book. I would appreciate it if you could leave your invaluable review on Amazon.com with your feedback. Thank you!